BUREAUCRATS, POLITICS, AND THE ENVIRONMENT

Bureaucrats, Politics, and the Environment

Richard W. Waterman, Amelia A. Rouse, and Robert L. Wright

With a contribution by Kenneth J. Meier

University of Pittsburgh Press

Published by the University of Pittsburgh Press, Pittsburgh, Pa., 15260

Library of Congress Cataloging-in-Publication Data

Waterman, Richard W.
  Bureaucrats, politics, and the environment / Richard W. Waterman,
Amelia A. Rouse, and Robert L. Wright ; with a contribution by Kenneth
J. Meier.
      p.   cm.
Includes bibliographical references and index.
  ISBN 0-8229-5829-5 (pbk. : alk. paper)
  1. Bureaucracy—United States—Case studies. 2. Environmental
agencies—United States—Case studies. 3. United States. Environmental
Protection Agency—Management. 4. New Mexico. Environment
Dept.—Management. I. Rouse, Amelia A. II. Wright, Robert (Robert Lee).
III. Title.
JF1501 .W37 2004
351'.01—dc22   2003015505

To Bertha and Bill Bureaucrat

CONTENTS

FIGURES AND TABLES

Figures

Tables

ACKNOWLEDGMENTS

This book began as a research project on the attitudes of bureaucrats and evolved through many stages into this book. Two of the chapters presented herein were published in quite different form in the *Journal of Public Administration Research and Theory*. We thank their editors and reviewers for many useful comments that helped us to improve our work. We also presented several chapters at professional forums such as the American Political Science Association, the Western Political Science Association, and the Midwest Political Science Association. We would like to thank the seemingly countless discussants, chairs, panelists, audience members, and other interested readers who were kind enough to review our work at various stages of development and to comment on it for us. Those comments greatly aided in the development of both our methodological and theoretical work. We also would like to thank the Institute for Public Policy at the University of New Mexico, which provided a best paper award that helped to fund one of our surveys. Additionally, we would like to thank Niels Aaboe of the University of Pittsburgh Press, and the anonymous reviewers, for greatly helping us to improve the manuscript. As a result of their comments and suggestions, this is a much more focused work.

We would also very much like to thank our boyfriends and girlfriends, who in the course of this long project became husbands, wives, and significant others, who stood by and watched (though apparently not with bated breath) as we wrote convention papers, journal articles, and eventually this work. Remarkably, we were able to finish all of these projects before either the Boston Red Sox or Chicago Cubs could win a single World Series. Who'd have thunk it?

ACRONYMS

CWA	Clean Water Act
DFA	Department of Finance and Administration
DMRs	Discharge Monitoring Reports
DOE	U.S. Department of Energy
EMS	Enforcement Management System
EPA	Environmental Protection Agency
FWPCA	Federal Water Pollution Control Act
HEW	Department of Health, Education, and Welfare
ICPSR	Inter-University Consortium for Political and Social Research
LFC	Legislative Finance Committee
MDS	multidimensional scaling
NMED	New Mexico Environment Department
NPEDS	National Pollutant Discharge Elimination Program
OMB	Office of Management and Budget
OSM	Office of Surface Mining
SIPs	State Implementation Plans
SRC	University of Michigan Survey Research Center
TVA	Tennessee Valley Authority
WIPP	Waste Isolation Pilot Program

BUREAUCRATS, POLITICS, AND THE ENVIRONMENT

1

~

Bureaucracy

Perceptions and Misperceptions

This is a book about bureaucratic theory. There are many theories of bureaucratic politics and yet few areas of agreement among them. For example, Woodrow Wilson (1987, 18) wrote, "administration lies outside the proper sphere of politics." While most scholars now agree that there is politics in administration (even Wilson concedes this point), the "politics-administration dichotomy" continues to be reflected in the debate over whether bureaucrats should be "responsive" to elected officials or "neutral competent" (see Moe 1985b; Heclo 1975). We also learn from the literature that the growth of bureaucratic power has created a "bureaucratic problem" (Wilson 1967), and that policy implementation by the bureaucracy is fraught with politics and usually fails (Moynihan 1969; Pressman and Wildavsky 1973; Mazmanian and Sabatier 1983).

With regard to the nature of bureaucratic politics, is it the politics of agency capture (Huntington 1952; Bernstein 1955), of cozy iron triangles (Cater 1964; Freeman 1965), and subsystem politics? If so, are such important constitutional actors as the president, the Congress (as a whole and not just its individual committees), and the courts mere bystanders without access or influence (see Lowi 1979; Noll 1971; Dodd and Schott 1979; Woll 1963)? Or are these same policy actors keenly involved in attempts at political control of the bureaucracy (Moe 1982, 1985a; Wood and Waterman 1991)? If so, is Congress the dominant actor in bureaucratic politics (Weingast and Moran 1983) or is it the president (Moe 1985b)? If either actor is dominant, then what influence do the courts exert (Melnick 1983; Moe 1985a; Wood and Waterman 1993)?

And what of the bureaucrats themselves: do they perform vitally important functions for society (Weber 1946) or are they primarily interested in shirking hierarchical attempts at political control (Mitnick 1980)? Are their behaviors best explained by an economic rather than a political model (Posner 1974), and if so, are they budget-maximizers (Niskanen 1971, 1975, 1991, 1994) or are they motivated by other goals including their own functional and solidary preferences (Downs 1967; Brehm and Gates 1993, 1999)? Do they have too much discretion (Galloway 1951; McConnell 1966; Stone 1977; Lowi 1979) or do they need discretion to carry out the law (Rourke 1984, 37; Davis 1969a, 1969b; Bardach and Kagan 1982; Kiewiet and McCubbins 1991)?

With regard to bureaucrats' relationship to their political principals, does an information asymmetry exist (Bendor, Taylor, and Van Gaalen 1985, 1987)? Are bureaucrats always in goal conflict with political principals (Waterman and Meier 1999)? Are agents mostly passive, choosing only to respond or not to principal political control stimuli, or are agents active, even influencing the principals that seek to control them (Krause 1999)?

In sum, if we read the entire bureaucratic literature, we will find that the answer to most of these questions is often both yes or no (and sometimes it depends) based on which source you consult. There is politics and there isn't. The president and Congress have influence and they do not. Iron triangles dominate and they are no longer relevant. Hence, it is difficult to glean definitive answers from the literature, in part because even prominent theories of the bureaucratic process (such as the principal-agent model and the budget-maximizing bureaucratic thesis) are driven by normative assumptions about the nature of bureaucrats.

These normative assumptions, in turn, have an impact on the answer to such big questions as: who is best suited to promote democratic values, bureaucrats or their elected political masters (Lowi 1979; Wood and Waterman 1991, 1994)? To a large extent the answer depends on a normative consideration: whom do you most trust, bureaucrats or elected officials? This may seem like an easy question (given all of the negative antibureaucratic rhetoric), but just think about the case of the Reagan administration and the Environmental Protection Agency (EPA) in the 1980s. Of the two, whom did you most trust to deal with environmental policy? The answer probably depends on whether you support vigorous environmental enforcement. If so, then you were more likely to trust the EPA (the bureaucracy) than the Reagan administration.

Our point is that if you look at the bureaucratic literature over the past century you will learn all sorts of contradictory things about bureaucrats, bureaucracy, and the institutions that interact with them. In fact, few governmental institutions have been the subject of more study and less understanding than the bureaucracy. As Meier (1992, 17) notes, "Of all U.S. political institutions, bureaucracy is by far the least known." This situation is perplexing, for as Woll (1963, vii) writes, "Virtually every aspect of our daily lives is regulated to some degree by one or the other of the numerous administrative agencies that make up the national bureaucracy." Peters (1984, 1) also comments, "Government is increasingly a part of the daily life of the average citizen." Likewise, Rourke (1976, 14) writes, "No modern state could operate for a day without the performance of a myriad of tasks by highly trained bureaucracies." Yet we can think of no other literature in which one political institution is described in such a bipolar fashion. Bureaucracy is both good and bad, necessary and wasteful, and, at its worst, a dangerous threat to our democratic way of life.

In this book we employ survey research techniques in an attempt to try to reconcile some of the many controversies and inconsistencies in the bureaucratic theory literature. We examine two sets of bureaucrats who are responsible for protecting the environment: enforcement personnel from the Office of Water of the EPA at the federal level, and employees of the New Mexico Environment Department (NMED) at the state level. A number of top-down studies of the bureaucracy have examined these bureaucrats in considerable detail (Wood 1988; Wood and Waterman 1991, 1993, 1994). It is our intention to bring another perspective to this debate by examining the perceptions of federal- and state-level environmental bureaucrats. Thus, we examine what these officials think about politics, the environment, their agency budgets, and the political officials and institutions with which they interact, including the regulated industry.

Everybody's Scapegoat

As we have noted, normative themes permeate the bureaucratic literature. To begin with, public and scholarly perceptions of the bureaucracy can be characterized as largely pejorative. Boyer (1964, vii) writes, "Only in the United States is 'bureaucracy' an ugly word." Likewise, Gormley (1989, 3) comments, "Bureaucracy has never been a popular institution in the United States, but for the last decades it has come under continual siege. Presidents, interest groups, members of Congress, and the public at large have blamed their problems on bureaucracy. At the same time that the bureaucracy serves as the political scapegoat in the United States, the expectations for and demands on bureaucracy continue to escalate."

Bureaucracy is everybody's scapegoat. If there is a problem in our society the quick and easy solution is to blame it on the bureaucracy. Why did the terrorist attacks of September 11, 2001 succeed? While there are many factors involved, we have learned that bureaucracies such as the Federal Bureau of Investigation, the National Security Agency, and the Central Intelligence Agency were unable to process and collate vital information in a timely fashion. In short, one explanation is that the bureaucracy let us down. Ironically, the solution is to create new bureaucracies such as the Department of Homeland Security and to federalize airport security, which creates yet another new layer of bureaucracy.

Terrorism is not the only area in which the bureaucracy has been found to be at fault. If the crime rate is too high, if the deficit is out of control, or if American businesses cannot compete with their foreign competitors, then politicians, the media, and many scholars blame the bureaucracy. Long gone are the days when a scholar of the reputation of Paul Appleby (1945) dedicated his book to "Bill Bureaucrat," the average, hard-working guy who toiled in the bureaucracy on our behalf. Today most polemics criticize bureaucrats and the bureaucracy for a lack of compassion (Thompson 1975), a rigid inability to change (Mazmanian and Neinaber 1979; Foster 1990), their immortality (Kaufman 1976), a lack of responsiveness to elected officials and the public (Dodd and Schott 1979), and even their tendency to subvert democratic principles (Lowi 1979).

In short, the overwhelming focus of the literature is on what is wrong with the bureaucracy. One clear consequence of this one-sided fo-

cus is that we have lost our sense of perspective: we no longer understand how or why bureaucracy fits into our overall governmental system.
For example, as Boyer (1964, vii) writes, we criticize the bureaucracy, yet
"curiously, the same persons and interests who complain about bureaucracy are those who by their demands on government help to make it
grow." When we demand a new prescription drug program or better airport security we tend to forget that it is inevitably the bureaucracy that
will implement these programs, and new programs create new bureaucracies with more bureaucrats.

Given our society's continuous demand for new programs, and
hence indirectly for new bureaucracies, why have politicians, the popular
press, and the public been so critical of the bureaucracy? One reason is
that few people make this obvious connection between programs and
bureaucracy. As importantly, there are few individuals who are willing to
defend the bureaucracy. Whereas the president and his/her advisers
speak for the presidency, representatives and senators speak for the Congress, and judges speak for the courts, no one speaks for the bureaucracy.
There is no high-profile Bill or Bertha Bureaucrat possessing the necessary credibility to defend the institution. Rather, most high-profile bureaucrats, such as the secretary of state or the chairman of the Federal
Reserve Board would be loath to even acknowledge that they are in fact
bureaucrats. While they can be counted on to defend their own agencies,
they cannot be expected to defend the bureaucracy as a whole. Because
there is no one willing to speak on its behalf, most people perceive the
bureaucracy as a faceless and highly impersonal entity, a point often em-
phasized in political stump speeches, as well as literature (e.g., George
Orwell's 1984) and film (Terry Gilliam's Brazil). In these accounts, the bureaucracy is represented as a cold, uncaring automaton that is unresponsive and impersonal.

Since no one represents the bureaucracy, it is highly susceptible to attack. Likewise, there is a clear incentive to bash the bureaucracy. As Wilson (1989, 236) notes, "No politician ever lost votes by denouncing the
bureaucracy." Likewise, Stanley Greenberg (1995, 281), formerly President Bill Clinton's chief pollster, comments, "Today, any party aspiring to
national leadership . . . will have to establish its bona fides as hostile to
bureaucracy . . ." As a result of such advice, many politicians eagerly take
up the cause, attacking the bureaucracy as bloated, unproductive, inefficient, and lumbering, among other pejorative terms. Politicians also

regularly accuse the bureaucracy of being out of touch and unresponsive to the public, charges they are, on occasion, guilty of themselves.

Politicians were not always so critical of the bureaucracy. Rather, this popular propensity to blame the bureaucracy surfaced during the late 1960s, largely as a response to the perceived failure of many of Lyndon Johnson's Great Society programs. As Pressman and Wildavsky (1973) and Moynihan (1969) ably demonstrate, many of the Great Society programs failed to achieve their basic objectives. President Johnson himself was aware of these problems and, as a result, established the President's Task Force on Government Organization. In its 1967 report, the committee reported, "Many domestic social programs are under severe attack. Some criticism is political. . . . Some criticism stems from deflated hopes, with current funding levels well below ultimate need and demand. Some criticism arises because of alleged organizational and managerial weakness. After several months of study, we believe the organizational criticism is merited."

The failure of many Great Society antipoverty programs, along with the Johnson administration's support for civil rights, prompted George Wallace to criticize the bureaucracy in his populist stump speeches during his 1968 third-party presidential campaign. As Theodore White (1969, 345) writes, "If George Wallace hates anything, it is not Negroes— it is the Federal government of the United States and its 'Pointy-head' advisers, the 'intellectual morons,' the 'guideline writers' of Washington who try to upset the natural relations of the races." Wallace's campaign, though replete with hot racial rhetoric, was well received by a significant portion of the American electorate, including many middle-class Americans (see Greenberg 1995). As a third-party candidate, Wallace won several southern states in the 1968 presidential campaign. He also did well in many northern suburban areas. Furthermore, four years later, at the time of the assassination attempt that effectively removed him from the 1972 presidential campaign, Wallace had won more primary votes than any of his Democratic opponents.

Therefore, even if Wallace's racial message was abhorrent, his antigovernment message was popular. As a result, other politicians soon adopted the Wallace strategy of bashing Washington bureaucrats. In the 1972 presidential election, it was Richard Nixon, the incumbent president, who co-opted Wallace's message. His law and order theme and his attacks on federally mandated busing borrowed generously from Wallace's anti-Washington rhetoric.

In recent decades, candidates of both political parties have adopted anti-Washington, antibureaucratic rhetoric as standard components of their stump speeches; in fact, the anti-Washington "outsider" image has become increasingly popular among presidential candidates of both major political parties (Waterman, Wright, and St. Clair 1999). Of these politicians, Ronald Reagan is perhaps best remembered for attacking the bureaucracy. Yet such ideologically diverse candidates for president as Gerald Ford, Jimmy Carter, and Edward Kennedy each found it palatable to do so. In 1992 all three presidential candidates, Bill Clinton, George Bush, and Ross Perot, attacked the bureaucracy in their standard campaign speeches. Only Ross Perot (1992), on occasion, was willing to compliment bureaucrats. For instance, he wrote, "The word 'bureaucrat' conjures up some bloodless, uncaring robot with a rubber stamp. In truth, I have found almost every federal employee I've encountered to be a dedicated, intelligent professional." The presidential campaigns of 1996 and 2000 likewise included copious anti-Washington and antibureaucratic references.

Politicians have not been the only policy actors to blame the bureaucracy for our nation's problems in recent years. The media also plays a prominent role. As Goodsell (1983, 2) writes, "As for portrayals in mass media, we encounter a relatively simple picture, confidently expressed. The employee of bureaucracy, that 'lowly bureaucrat,' is seen as lazy or snarling, or both. The office occupied by this pariah is viewed as bungling or inhumane, or both. The overall edifice of bureaucracy is pictured as overstaffed, inflexible, unresponsive, and power-hungry, all at once. These images are agreed upon by writers and groups of every shade of opinion. One is hard pressed to think of a concept more deeply ingrained and widely expressed in American cultural life."

What evidence has the media used to come to this critical conclusion about the bureaucracy? Goodsell (1983, 3) continues, "One source the popular critics always draw upon is that item found in almost every edition of every daily newspaper, the bureaucratic horror story." Goodsell describes these stories as a "graphic and sympathetic account of how some poor citizen has been mistreated by incompetent bureaucrats or how in some other way a great bureaucratic error has been committed."

Politicians and other decision makers then focus on these accounts. One can speculate that when a citizen hears a bureaucratic horror story from an official as prominent as the president of the United States, it lends considerable credibility to the account, even if it is an isolated incident and therefore not generalizable, and even if the facts of the particular incident are still in question.

In addition to bureaucratic horror stories, editorial writers and other exalted purveyors of common wisdom have expressed pejorative opinions about the bureaucracy. For example, George Will, in evaluating President Bill Clinton's 1993 plan to reduce the deficit, concluded, "how advanced is a project if bureaucrats in Washington can fathom it?" (1993, 68). When we add to this mix such popular radio and television pundits as Rush Limbaugh on the right and Howard Stern on the left, who likewise profit at the expense of the bureaucracy, there is clearly no reason to believe that bureaucracy will be presented in a more popular light by the mass media anytime soon.

As a result, it is not surprising to find that most Americans hold negative opinions of the bureaucracy. An analysis of public opinion data provides some evidence in this regard. In a poll reported by Larry Hill (1989), 78 percent of the respondents to a 1973 University of Michigan Survey Research Center (SRC) poll agreed, "too many government agencies do the same thing." Likewise, 58 percent expressed the opinion that bureaucrats "gain the most from government services." More than half said that bureaucrats do not take responsibility for anything and nearly one-half agreed that bureaucrats are not interested in the problems of ordinary people. Substantial percentages also believed that bureaucrats pry into their personal lives and use their authority to push people around (see also Hill, Wamsley, and Goodsell 1992).

In contrast, however, 71 percent of the respondents to an early 1980s poll conducted by the *Washington Post* said that they were pleased with their interactions with federal agencies (Hill 1989, 7). While 78 percent of the respondents to the SRC poll believed that "too many government agencies do the same thing," 72 percent also expressed the opinion that "government workers work hard and try to do a good job." Likewise, 68 percent of the respondents said, "governmental workers are usually very helpful" (Hill 1989). These findings suggest that the public holds both highly positive and negative assessments of the bureaucracy simultaneously. Thus, as Wilson (1989, x) writes:

[handwritten in left margin: General public / Perception of bureaucrat]

Citizens and taxpayers have their own global view of bureaucracy. To them, bureaucrats are lethargic, incompetent hacks who spend their days spinning out reels of red tape and reams of paperwork, all the while going to great lengths to avoid doing the job they were hired to do. Their agencies chiefly produce waste, fraud, abuse, and mismanagement. That this view is an exaggeration is readily shown by public-opinion surveys in which people are asked about their personal experiences with government agencies. The great majority of the respondents say that these experiences were good, that the agency personnel were helpful, friendly, and competent. This can only mean that those lazy, incompetent bureaucrats must work for some other agency—the one the citizen never sees.

How can we reconcile these contradictory results from various public opinion polls? Hill (1989, 1–2) suggests an answer. He argues that the public has not made a sufficient effort to understand the bureaucracy:

> I assume that one of the most conspicuous developments of recent decades is the growth of government and specifically the emergence of large public bureaucracies as important political actors. Furthermore, I believe that the American public has, in general, neglected to integrate this development into its overall understanding of the political process. Most Americans have failed to take bureaucracy seriously: they have not understood bureaucracy in relation to their own demands, priorities, and preparedness to assume the tasks of governance . . . [Rather in] the post-war period, deploring bureaucracy has become an increasingly popular national pastime.

There is another possible answer, however, which is that rather than the public's lack of effort, contradictory public attitudes may be related to the mixed signals the public receives. On the one hand, the public hears from the politicians and the press that the bureaucratic process is the root of many of society's problems. On the other hand, the public, in general, is satisfied with its individual contacts with bureaucracy. Given the nature of the evidence the public receives, we should expect the public to be confused.

Unfortunately, there is little prospect that the signals the public receives will become more consistent in the future. It is likewise difficult to imagine that positive stories about the bureaucracy would sell newspapers or attract large ratings on programs such as *60 Minutes, 20/20,* or *Dateline*. These programs enjoy high ratings when they expose bureaucratic incompetence, not the reverse. In essence, then, there is a self-serving bias in the political arena and in the media against bureaucracy. We do not hear many positive assessments about bureaucracy, nor should we expect to. The clear incentive is and will remain to bash the bureaucracy despite occasional empirical evidence that the increasing size and representativeness of the bureaucracy actually is related to positive policy outcomes (see Meier, Polinard, and Wrinkle 2000; Hindera 1993).

The Bureaucrats Speak for Themselves

We conducted two surveys in the mid- to late 1990s, one of personnel working for the National Pollutant Discharge Elimination System (NPDES), the surface water enforcement division of the EPA, and one of all environmental personnel working for the NMED. In this book we analyze these two surveys and apply the results to a diverse set of questions promoted by bureaucratic literatures, such as whether the bureaucracy is too liberal or too conservative and whether bureaucrats have too much discretion. Our primary concern, however, is with the two currently dominant theories of the bureaucratic process: the principal-agent model (see Moe 1982, 1985a; Wood 1988; Hedge, Scicchitano, and Metz 1991) and the theory of the budget-maximizing bureaucrat (Niskanen 1971). We will critique both of these theories and then examine how our survey results reflect on their basic assumptions.

We focus on environmental agencies because they have been the topic of much past research on bureaucratic politics (see Wood 1988; Wood and Waterman 1991, 1993). Our focus on environmental agencies allows us to examine agencies that have a direct daily impact on the quality of our lives. We also think that a focus on two environmental agencies is appropriate because the Environmental Protection Agency and the New Mexico Environment Department are the subject of the same kinds of perceptions and misperceptions that we have identified. Some people vilify them while others believe they perform a vital function. What then are the basic characteristics of these two agencies?

The Environmental Protection Agency

The Environmental Protection Agency was established by President Richard Nixon via executive order on December 2, 1970, combining a number of federal programs dealing with air pollution from the Department of Health, Education, and Welfare (HEW); water pollution from the Department of the Interior and HEW; solid waste management from HEW; and radiation standards from the Atomic Energy Commission. The new EPA also replaced the National Air Pollution Control Administration, which had been the federal government's primary environmental management agency (see appendix). As Landy, Roberts, and Thomas (1994, 32) write, from Nixon's "point of view, creating a new agency had two very attractive features. First, it was a highly visible innovative action. Second, it represented a compromise between those who wanted to totally redesign the executive branch and those who wanted to change nothing."

The EPA is the largest of the federal regulatory agencies. It administers more than two dozen statutes and has some eighteen thousand employees, approximately twelve thousand of them working in one of its ten regional offices. Among its employees are a large number of scientists, engineers, attorneys, and other professionals. In fact, the EPA has distinguished itself by acquiring an impressive cadre of experts on environmental affairs, and many of them are strong advocates of environmental protection. As we shall see, however, it would be a mistake to assume that the EPA personnel constitute a monolith in support of a specific environmental or political approach.

Overseeing the agency is the EPA administrator, who is selected by and serves at the pleasure of the president. To increase presidential influence, the administrator's term was designed to run concurrently with the president's. To ensure that the administrator would be accountable to the public and environmentalists, Senate confirmation was required. The administrator was endowed with a great deal of authority and, perhaps more importantly, a great deal of discretion, extending from rulemaking to the authority to reorganize the EPA's offices and to develop the agency's budget. Still, the administrator does not work alone. In addition to a deputy administrator and the heads of various offices (e.g., the Office of Water or Office of Air, Noise, and Radiation), the administrator also shares responsibility with regional administrators, one for each of the agency's ten regional offices.

The ability to reorganize the EPA and the ability to control budget allocations to the regional offices are the main centralized powers of the EPA administrator. Indeed, upon appointment by President Bill Clinton, Carol Browner proceeded to change the EPA from a set of media-specific departments (i.e., water and air division, etc.) to industry-based multimedia divisions (this process was still in the planning stages during our data collection). The strong central powers of the EPA administrator, however, are somewhat mitigated by the fact that there are ten diverse regional offices run by administrators who are chosen through the political practice of senatorial courtesy. These regional administrators often demonstrate considerable autonomy from the EPA's central office in Washington, even disagreeing with goals and objectives. As was explained to us by a former head of the Office of Water, while the regional administrators are technically under the control of the administrator, they exhibit a great deal of discretion in terms of how they run their offices. In fact, we were told that some regional administrators were more responsive to regional and local concerns than they were to the dictates of the EPA administrator. The diversity across the ten regional offices of the EPA also is related to geographically based interests and needs, the variety of federal-state power sharing arrangements, and the expertise and priorities of the regional administrators. For example, region two covers New Jersey, New York (regional offices), Puerto Rico, and the Virgin Islands, all of whose administrators have primacy over their NPDES programs. This region's primary concerns are problems associated with heavily populated areas, such as inadequate waste disposal plans that lead to ground water contamination. Region eight covers Colorado (regional offices), Montana, North Dakota, South Dakota (the only non-primacy state in the region), Utah, and Wyoming. This is an area in which who gets water is among the top concerns of regional administrators; water pollution concerns in this region stem primarily from agriculture and mining (Hunter and Waterman 1992, 1996). Historically, the regional offices of New York and Boston (region one) have had such a great influence over the development and content of water pollution regulations that NPDES permit holders or permittees (discharges into surface waterways are not legal without a permit) and EPA personnel in the western and northwest regions claim that the NPDES laws have an eastern bias and do not address adequately the needs of their regions.

As we shall see, NPDES enforcement personnel perceive their regional administrator as one of the most influential forces in determining how they perform their jobs. It follows, then, that the interests and abilities of those appointed as regional administrators add important elements to the diversity of regional NPDES enforcement. Arguably, the political nature of the appointment of the ten regional administrators allows regional concerns to be articulated and addressed more appropriately than would a centralized, Washington, D.C.–based institution. This institutional configuration, however, leads to broad discretion in the interpretation and enforcement of the NPDES regulations.

Another factor that complicates EPA enforcement is that the agency is not the only one responsible for the development of environmental policy; as many as a dozen other federal agencies share jurisdiction with the EPA on various regulatory issues. In some cases, the EPA is even responsible for regulating other agencies, such as the Tennessee Valley Authority (TVA). In addition to interagency regulatory activity, the EPA must also cooperate with the fifty states in the development of regulatory policy. Under the provisions of the Clean Air Act of 1970, states must submit State Implementation Plans (SIPs) to the Environmental Protection Agency. These plans suggest the method by which state governments will comply with the standards and deadlines enumerated in the act. The EPA then must review the SIPs to determine if they adequately meet federal guidelines. Although this review process gives the EPA oversight authority over state environmental agencies, it does not guarantee control. As a number of EPA personnel told us, the agency does not have enough personnel or sufficient resources to perform a comprehensive study of every state's environmental program (Hunter and Waterman 1992, 1996).

As a result, much authority is necessarily delegated to the states. Ann O'M. Bowman (1984, 1985a, 1985b) argues that this intergovernmental component of environmental regulation impedes progress in implementing environmental programs. Coordination of decision making is more difficult because different levels of government and governmental agencies are involved. Yet as Gormley (1987, 285) notes, over the past two decades, "the federal government has delegated considerable authority over environmental protection to the states." In particular, during Ann Gorsuch Burford's tenure as EPA administrator (1981–1983) "state program responsibilities grew from 33 percent of possible assumptions of responsibility to 66 percent" (Gormley 1987, 285). State involvement in environmental protection continued to grow after Burford's departure.

In short, the EPA is a curious blend of centralized control (held primarily by its administrator) and decentralized authority over its many functional responsibilities, the other federal agencies with which it shares responsibility, and the intergovernmental component of environmental regulation. These features make it a particularly interesting agency to examine in the context of the principal-agent model, which focuses on information asymmetries and goal conflict.

Specifically, the EPA personnel we interviewed enforce the provisions of the Clean Water Act of 1972 (and its amendments) under the NPDES. The NPDES program is one of three permit programs created under the provisions of the Clean Water Act of 1972. It was designed to oversee point source discharges by municipalities and industrial firms, among other polluters.

The NPDES Program

The Federal Water Pollution Control Act (FWPCA) of 1972, more familiarly known as the Clean Water Act (CWA) was offered as the legislative solution to the uneven and ineffective water protection programs of the past. Passed by Congress over Nixon's veto, the CWA's stated objective was "to restore and maintain the chemical, physical and biological integrity of the nation's waters" (Arbuckle 1993, 155). The act's basic goal was to regulate every pollutant or contaminant discharged by facilities into the nation's waters.

The cornerstone of the CWA was the creation of the National Pollutant Discharge Elimination System as the permitting and enforcement body for some sixty thousand conditional authorizations to discharge. Industry-by-industry standards were to be set based on the best available pollution control technology, with consideration given to the cost of implementation to the regulated industries. Industries were required to apply for discharge permits, to confirm compliance, and to report noncompliance to the sovereign agency. NPDES monitoring and reporting functions (whether EPA or state controlled) include: creation and enforcement of compliance schedules, setting effluent limitations, re-permitting, and permit revocation. Enforcement tools available under the NPDES range from warning letters to criminal lawsuits.

The responsibility for the development and enforcement of nationwide water-quality standards was assigned to the nascent Environmental Protection Agency. The CWA also created a means by which, under specified circumstances, states could take control of permitting and enforcement tasks. In these primacy states the EPA acts in an oversight capacity.

Under the CWA the EPA is responsible for ensuring that the system's provisions and their enforcement are applied in a generally even and consistent manner across the nation to achieve the fair treatment under the law of all permittees that receive NPDES permits under the program. Toward that end, each state agency and EPA regional office must adhere to the Enforcement Management System (EMS). There is, however, no single "correct" EMS, but each region must establish within acceptable parameters procedures for the tracking of compliance, and for enforcement actions regarding permittees. The purpose of allowing each region and primacy state to develop its own specific EMS is to reflect the wide variations across states and regions with regard to organizational structures, staffing, and water problems, while effectively incorporating the basic principles of the NPDES. For this reason, the organizational structure of NPDES personnel varies from one EPA region to another.

The structure of regional offices is not at all standardized; there is no "standard" location for the system's compliance officials within regional hierarchies. In most cases, the program is part of the water management section. In one case (region seven) it is located in a separate enforcement division. These differences in Enforcement Management Systems also contribute to increased bureaucratic discretion. The parameters of that discretion vary across the ten regions.

The EMS for each region specifies how compliance information is to be maintained and translated into enforcement action. Inventories are kept of each permittee's discharge limits, compliance dates, and effluent data through the Permit Compliance System. Permits are reviewed at established intervals, and can be subject to modification. All permittees must regularly submit Discharge Monitoring Reports (DMRs). Pre-enforcement screenings are conducted to review permittees' records and behavior, and to identify noncompliant permittees for possible enforcement action. The EMS for a region also establishes procedures for an enforcement evaluation when an incident of noncompliance is identified. The evaluation determines what enforcement action, if any, is appropriate to the specific circumstances. The procedure may allow for no enforcement action to be taken if an investigation indicates none is warranted. Field investigations (inspections) are an integral part of the enforcement program and are conducted both routinely and by the special efforts of field units. Although investigations are supposed to be conducted every year, they can be initiated at any time in the enforcement evaluation process. The response to a violation might be informal or formal, such as a phone call, an administrative order to respond or abate, or a judicial referral to the U.S. Department of Justice or the state attorney general.

New Mexico Environment Department

As noted above, the states also play an important role in environmental protection. We therefore examined the perceptions of state-level bureaucrats at the New Mexico Environment Department. According to the NMED's Web site, "The Department's mission is to provide the highest quality of life throughout the state by promoting a safe, clean, and productive environment." Administratively, the NMED's secretary reports directly to the governor of New Mexico. According to the Web site, "The Office of the Secretary is responsible for departmental organization, staffing, budgeting and policies that enforce the laws and regulations which the department administers." Among the programs administered by the NMED are the Air Quality Bureau, the Occupational Health and Safety Bureau, the Solid Waste Bureau, the Underground Storage Tank Bureau, the Field Operations Division, the Drinking Water Bureau, and the Community Service Bureau.

The mission of the Air Quality Bureau is "to prevent the decline of air quality in areas that are presently relatively pollution free, and to direct the clean-up of the air in areas which currently do not meet minimum standards." The Occupational Health and Safety Bureau assures "every employee safe and healthful working conditions by providing for: "the establishment of occupational health and safety regulations applicable to places of employment in this state," as well as "the effective enforcement of the health and safety regulations, education and training programs for employers and employees in recognition of their responsibilities under the Occupational Health and Safety Act, and advice and assistance to them about effective means of preventing occupational injuries and illnesses." The Solid Waste Bureau assures "solid waste is managed in such a way as to minimize impact on the environment and public health," while the Underground Storage Tank Bureau seeks to "reduce, mitigate and eliminate the threats to the environment posed by petroleum products or hazardous material or wastes released from underground storage tanks."

The Field Operations Division of the NMED, according to the Web site,

> conducts its diverse programs through offices in twenty-two cities representing a geographical and demographic cross-section of the state. The field offices are divided into four districts with boundaries that generally depict the four quadrants of the state. . . . The majority of the Field Operation Division's work is concentrated in seven programs. The Drinking Water Bureau coordinates drinking water supplies. The Community Service Bureau coordinates the remaining six programs: Liquid Waste, Food Service and Processors, Public Swimming Pool and Public Bath Safety and Sanitation, Vector Control (plague, hantavirus, and other vector-borne diseases) and more recently, the Radiation Protection Program and WIPP (Waste Isolation Pilot Program) Emergency Response Training Program. Additionally the field offices review plans and specifications for proposed water supply systems and wastewater treatment systems. The division also assists counties in the planning and review process for subdivision development. In this capacity, staff provides input in the areas of water quality, and the disposal of liquid and solid waste.

The mission of the division is to facilitate the programs and other activities directed from the central office in Santa Fe, New Mexico. To do this the division operations include "administrative supervision of field efforts in the Underground Storage Tank, Hazardous and Radioactive Waste, Air Quality, Surface Water, Ground Water and Solid Waste Programs."

The groundwater division's goal is "to protect ground water quality and minimize existing and potential ground water contamination." The Hazardous Waste Bureau regulates "all present hazardous waste management activities in order to prevent environmental degradation," while the Surface Water Division protects "the quality of surface waters (lakes, streams, and wetlands)."

Consequently, while the EPA enforcement personnel we interviewed worked only in the field of the surface water division (NPDES), the NMED personnel work in a wide variety of environmental protection fields. Before turning to an analysis of the individuals who work in these agencies, we next address the scholarly literature on bureaucracy.

Principal-Agent Models

A Theoretical Cul-de-Sac

Richard W. Waterman and Kenneth J. Meier

Theory is at the heart of the debate over the nature of bureaucratic politics. A primary target of this debate is the principal-agent model of political control of the bureaucracy. While principal-agent models originally derived from law and economics, they have become the basis for an extensive set of studies relating bureaucracy to elected officials (e.g., Mitnick 1980; Moe 1982, 1985a; Scholz and Wei 1986; Wood 1988, 1990; Wood and Waterman 1991, 1994). Such models also have been extended to presidents' decisions to use force (Downs and Rocke 1994) and the Supreme Court and its relationship to lower courts (Songer, Segal, and Cameron 1994). Our objective is to examine principal-agent theory critically, analyze its theoretical range, relax some of its restrictive assumptions, and, in the process, present a more general theoretical framework of relationships between bureaucracy and its political environment. Although our critique may be relevant for other uses of the principal-agent model, we limit our assessment to its use as an empirical theory of bureaucracy.

The Principal-Agent Model

Our primary concern is that, despite the widespread referencing of the principal-agent model, only in rare instances does a researcher actually discuss the model and how its assumptions fit the problem to be studied (such instances include Mitnick 1980 and Moe 1982, 1985a, 1987). The model, itself, derives from accounting, law, and economics and is essentially a theory about contractual relationships between buyers and sellers (see Pratt and Zeckhauser 1985). According to Perrow (1986, 224), "In its simplest form, agency theory assumes that social life is a series of contracts. Conventionally, one member, the 'buyer' of goods or services is designated the 'principal,' and the other, who provides the goods or service is the 'agent'—hence the term 'agency theory.' The principal-agent relationship is governed by a contract specifying what the agent should do and what the principal must do in return."

A common application in economics is the market for professional services, say between a patient and a physician (Evans 1980). Assuming both are rational utility maximizers, a patient and a physician are likely to have different goals. A patient would like to be made healthy but pay as little as possible. A physician would be interested in maximizing income, so faces the temptation to provide more medical services than are necessary or to charge a higher price than is warranted. In this exchange, patients are at a disadvantage because they cannot directly evaluate the services provided by the physician. In short, an information asymmetry exists with an advantage to the physician. The principal seeks to manipulate and mold the behavior of the agent so that he/she will act in a manner consistent with the principal's preferences. The contractual arrangement is one tool for accomplishing this goal.

Initially, the theory appears to have some application in studying relationships between politicians (principals) and the bureaucracy (agents). Politicians and bureaucrats do not necessarily share similar goals. If we assume that they are rational utility maximizers (politicians maximizing reelection chances and bureaucrats maximizing budgets), politicians have an interest in policies that benefit their constituents but have no interest in paying excessively for them. Because politicians and political coalitions change over time and bureaucracies develop separate interests through institutionalization and changing external relationships, a potential conflict occurs where the goals and objectives of principals and agents are at odds.

Over time, politicians may seek to alter established policy toward their preferred objectives that may or may not be the same as those of the original legislation or political coalition. Bureaucracies, however, are more likely to be bound by past coalitions and legislation, putting them at odds with current politicians. Bureaucratic interests also diverge from the original policy through time as bureaucrats develop expertise about how the policy should be implemented or gain support from constituencies that favor different approaches. Even if no policy disagreement exists, principal-agent theory suggests that bureaucrats are likely to shirk, to produce outputs at a higher-than-needed cost or to produce a lower-than-desired level of outputs.

Agency theory posits a dynamic process of interaction between principals and agents, developing through time. In this process, bureaucrats have distinct information and expertise advantages over politicians. They better understand the policy and the organizational procedures required to implement it. So they have both the opportunity and the incentive to manipulate politicians and processes for political gain (see Niskanen 1971). For some policies, especially those of a technical nature, bureaucracies are more certain about organizational needs, so politicians are reluctant to intervene. The key question for agency theory, then, is how can politicians vested with contemporaneous legitimacy overcome these uncertainties and the bureaucracy's inherent tendency to shirk (Wood and Waterman 1994)?

The information asymmetry between the principal and agent is at the heart of this question (Bendor, Taylor, and Van Gaalen 1985, 1987; Banks and Weingast 1992), as is uncertainty by the bureaucracy about the politician's level of attention. As Perrow (1986, 224) observes, "the principal-agent model is fraught with the problems of cheating, limited information, and bounded rationality in general." Hence, if the preferences of principals and agents diverge, if there is uncertainty between actors, and if the agent has a distinct information advantage, the probability of shirking increases. Under these circumstances, the principal must reduce uncertainty by acquiring offsetting information.

Given these problems, how, according to agency theory, can principals control bureaucratic agents? The answer is threefold. First, principal control is possible because elected officials create bureaucracies in the first place. They can design them with various incentive structures to facilitate control (McCubbins, Noll, and Weingast 1987, 1989; Potoski 2002; Whitford 2002; Lewis 2003; though Balla 1998 finds no empirical support for the "stacking the deck" thesis). Second, political principals also monitor the activities of their bureaucratic agents (Waterman and Wood 1993). Third, when bureaucratic activities stray from the principals' preferences, policy makers can then apply sanctions or rewards to bring agents back into line (McCubbins, Noll and Weingast 1987, 1989).

Goal conflict and information asymmetry are the two spark plugs that power the principal-agent theory. Because there is goal conflict between principals and agents, agents have the incentive to shirk (or engage in other non-sanctioned actions). The information asymmetry, in turn, gives bureaucrats the ability to be unresponsive to agents. Even in a case of relatively similar goals, conflict may exist over the exact means to use with an agent's desire to obtain slack resources, providing the incentive to shirk.

While this principal-agent model has been well articulated, and its key assumptions have been examined in disciplines such as economics (see Grossman and Hart 1983; Radner 1985; Singh 1985; Sappington 1991; Sinclair-Desgagne 1994), it has seldom been directly tested by political scientists, though there are exceptions. Brehm and Gates (1993; 1999, 3) empirically examine the propensity of bureaucrats to work, shirk, or commit sabotage and find that functional preferences ("the extent to which bureaucrats enjoy doing their job"), rather than oversight by supervisors, is the greatest constraint against shirking. Hammond and Miller (1985) and Bawn (1995) examine the role of expertise/information in relationship to institutional designs and administrative procedures and Balla and Wright (2001) examine how Congress controls the flow of information to the bureaucracy through the use of advisory committees. While there is some interesting work then, in general, there has been relatively little attention paid to the theory's key elements. Both information and goal conflict are treated as constants in the model with little change over time or across settings. As a result, the theory becomes static rather than dynamic and may force the analyst to frame questions in an inappropriate manner.

Information Asymmetry and Goal Conflict as Variables

Following Gormley (1986), who examined variations in regulatory politics according to different levels of salience and complexity, our first modification of principal-agent models is to relax the assumptions of an information asymmetry and goal conflict. We seek to treat these concepts as variables rather than as constants.

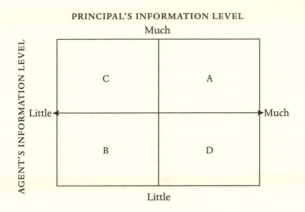

Information Asymmetry

Information asymmetry is simply the claim that agents possess greater information than principals. In a sense, the assumption is the combination of two variables—the information possessed by the agent and the information possessed by the principal. As shown in figure 2.1, when these variables are arrayed in two dimensions, the standard form of information asymmetry is only one of four possible situations.[1] Case A exists when both principal and agent possess a great deal of information, case B when neither possesses information, case C when the principal possesses a great deal of information but the agent does not, and case D when the agent possesses a great deal of information and the principal does not.

Case D represents the traditional information asymmetry of principal-agent models whereby a regulatory bureaucrat knows a great deal about a policy under consideration and the politician lacks this information. Should it, however, be modeled as the sole possible information relationship between principals and agents or do we have evidence from the literature suggesting that the other potential situations in figure 2.1 also exist? Clearly some case A situations exist in which both the principal and the agent are extremely well informed about the process; the 1993–1994 health care debate had a variety of political principals and bureaucratic agents involved, and both kinds of parties had access to information. It is also possible to conceive of situations in which both the politicians and the bureaucrats lack information (case B). In *The Politics of Sin*, Meier (1994) argues that drug policies generally fail because policy relevant information is not brought to bear; the law enforcement bureaucracies lack the capacity for policy analysis, and politicians have little interest in information that contradicts their view of the world. An information asymmetry does not exist in either case A or case B, yet these two cases are definitely distinct, since in one, information appears valuable and in the other it does not.

The most interesting possibility is case C, in which politicians have substantial information and bureaucrats have little. Such situations exist in large organizations where line bureaucrats perform such specialized jobs that they cannot see how their jobs contribute to what the organization does overall. Only their hierarchical superiors (their principals) have the viewpoints to see the entire range of operations. In regard to politicians and bureaucrats, such a situation might exist between politicians directing foreign policy and the military commander of a local naval base. The base commander is exposed to only a small part of the overall military policy plan and, therefore, is at an information disadvantage relative to his political superiors.

We do not argue that each of these cases is equally likely to occur. Given the development of administrative capacity and the characteristics of bureaucracy (specialization, professionalization, long time frames, etc.) bureaucracies are much more likely to gain information than politicians (Rourke 1984; Meier 1993). So cases A and D are probably more likely than B and C, but cases B and C do exist; most principal-agent studies have not recognized them because they have examined well-established, regulatory agencies at the federal level.

Goal Conflict

Because accounting and economics are based on scarcity and law is based on advocacy, it is inevitable for goal conflict to be part of any principal-agent theory.[2] Each discipline simply assumes conflict, and without conflict would have little to offer theoretically. Goal conflict, however, can readily be a variable, rather than a mere constant. Many relationships are based on cooperation rather than conflict, and the same should be true in bureaucratic-political relations (see Johnson 1993). The consideration of cooperative relationships between bureaucrats and politics was a prevalent theme in past regulatory policy literature. Indeed, the major criticism of regulatory policy from the 1930s through the 1960s (and continuing, in some cases, to the present) was that members of Congress, regulatory bureaucrats, and regulated interests formed cooperative iron triangles that dominated regulatory policy to the exclusion of the general public (Bernstein 1955; McConnell 1966; Herring 1967; Fellmuth 1970; Lowi 1979). That economics-oriented scholars would not notice this co-operative environment is more surprising given that George Stigler's (1970) generalization of this criticism spawned a significant research effort in economics (Posner 1974; Peltzman 1976; MacAvoy 1979; Noll and Owen 1983) and was a key work cited in his Nobel Prize.

Combining Information and Goals as Variables

Goal conflict can be combined with information as shown in figure 2.2. Again we dichotomize the variables for simplicity of presentation. We

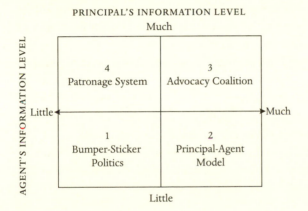

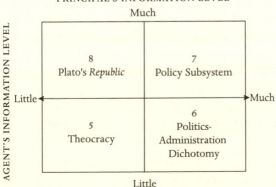

Figure 2.2: Combining Goals and Information

will examine this figure on a cell-by-cell basis to demonstrate that these cases actually exist. In the process we will offer some hypotheses based on the various combinations.

Case 1. Bumper-Sticker Politics: Goal Conflict, Principal and Agent Lack Information

In situations with goal conflict but little information possessed by politicians and bureaucrats, the bureaucratic role will become passive and clerical in nature.

This situation occurs when two or more advocacy coalitions argue about policy based on ideology; we call this bumper-sticker politics. Some likely cases are policies on school prayer, abortion, and early school desegregation. In these situations all knowledge is discounted and not part of the debate; it devolves to "it's our right" versus "you're killing babies." This is pure redistributive policy without any policy information to temper it.

In such situations bureaucrats really have no productive role. If they participate in the political debate, they are one interest among many. Bureaucrats are likely to be distrusted by at least one side of the debate; if that side wins, effort will be made to remove bureaucrats from the process with symbolic self-implementing policies ("you may pray in school"). Politicians will remain active in implementation with bureaucrats performing the role of clerks. This scenario is more feasible at the local level than the federal level.

Case 2: Classic Principal-Agent Model: Goal Conflict, Agent Has Information Advantage over Principal

This is the classic case of a principal-agent relationship. The relationship between President Reagan and most federal regulatory agencies followed this pattern; in fact, this pattern may be generalizable to many relationships between regulatory agencies and presidents. Since we already have discussed the theory earlier in this chapter we do not examine it further here.

Case 3. Advocacy Coalition: Goal conflict, Both Agent and Principal Have Information

In a situation of goal conflict with principals and agents both possessing information, relationships with political opponents will fit a principal-agent model and relationships with political supporters will fit a cooperative model with the bureaucrats as junior partners. The political skills of the bureaucrats become paramount in such relationships since they have to establish supporting coalitions and play off opponents with supporters.

In a case like this, bureaucracy becomes one political actor among many; it does not have any claim to sole expertise. Since there is no monopoly on information, the politics in these situations will resemble advocacy coalitions with bureaucrats and politicians aligned on both sides of the issue (Sabatier and Jenkins-Smith 1993). In such cases information is important, but the politics is the politics of ideas, and information is used in support of those ideas (Derthick and Quirk 1985). Major disputes in environmental policy (e.g., the Clean Air Act of 1990) and financial deregulation fit this pattern. Bureaucrats, although they might be from different agencies, can be on both sides of a policy dispute. This means that bureaucrats will be in competitive situations with other bureaucrats (law enforcement versus health care in alcohol-related problems; incentives versus "command and control" in environmental policy). Bureaucrats will have the classic principal-agent relationship with some politicians (those on the other side) and a cooperative relationship with others (those on their side; see the discussion of multiple principals below).

Case 4. Patronage System: Goal Conflict, Principals Have Information but Agents Do Not

In situations of goal conflict where principals have an information advantage, bureaucrats will be in the role of personal staff to the politicians. Bureaucratic resistance will be limited to rigidly carrying out policies (that is, administration by the rule book)

In this situation, politicians will dominate any relationship with bureaucrats since they both have legitimacy and knowledge. Political-bureaucratic relationships in patronage systems (especially in less developed countries) had these characteristics since bureaucrats were not perceived as having any special knowledge (White 1954). The bureaucracy in this situation serves as personal staff for the politicians. This pattern of relationships is also likely to occur in debates over privatization (any knowledge of the bureaucrats will be discounted as self-serving), occupational regulation reform (such as the regulation of barbers and similar occupations), and perhaps some civilian-military relationships (where knowledge is conceded only on tactics, not strategy).

Case 5: Theocracy: Goal Consensus, Principal and Agent Lack Information

In situations with goal consensus where neither the principal nor the agent possess information, the role of the bureaucrat will be as a supportive cheerleader. After policy adoption, the role of the bureaucrat will be to protect turf and joyfully implement policy.

In many areas of morality politics, goals are shared but neither the principal nor the agent has information, or both discount the value of information in the process. Everyone, for example, opposes drunk driving. When such issues become salient, the general strategy is for policy entrepreneurs to grab whatever ideas are floating around and adopt them. This permits the politician to take credit for combating the problem. Bureaucrats in these policy areas become advocates or perhaps, more harshly, cheerleaders. We perceive that this combination of goal consensus and lack of information characterizes current crime policies, tort reform in small states, drunk-driving policy, and drug control efforts (Meier 1994, 1988).

This case is normatively important because it produces policies that are not informed by policy analysis. As a result, such policies rarely work. The role of the bureaucrat becomes one of expanding and protecting turf, since to question the policy would be to challenge the goal consensus shared with the principal. Implementation in these cases can involve discretion; however, that discretion is generally unrelated to overall policy. Meier (1994) has characterized this relationship as a water faucet. Politicians can control the level of bureaucratic outputs by controlling resources. They control the level of enforcement, but not which individuals bear the brunt of enforcement. The latter will depend on how easy the law is to enforce. The agent will seek to maximize enforcement since this makes both the agent and the principal look good. Easy cases will take precedent over difficult cases; common cases will take precedent over unusual cases. With goal consensus there is little political monitoring of agents, so corruption in enforcement is common. The only critical information introduced in the debate in case 5 situations will come from agents who are not part of the regular policy system.

Case 6. Politics-Administration Dichotomy: Goal Consensus, Information Asymmetry Favors Agent

In areas with goal consensus but information asymmetry that favors the agent, bureaucrats will become technocrats and form relationships with principals that resemble those of the mythical politics-administration dichotomy.

When the agent and principal share goals but the agent possesses a great deal of information that the principal does not, we have the classic case of the politics-administration dichotomy. Khademian (1995) refers to agencies in this position as bottom-line agencies. Agencies are delegated a task with a clear goal and simply left alone as long as no major disasters happen.

A good example is the farm credit system. The goal of extending credit to the agricultural sector at low but economically sound rates is shared by the principals (members of Congress) and their agents (the Farm Credit System). Since the implementation of farm credit policies is complex, yet the success of the agency is apparent (total loans, net operating balances), agents are generally left alone by principals. Principals require regular reports, and if nothing is out of line, do nothing. Only when major problems occur do the principals intervene and try to take corrective action. Corrections are rare and tend to fix the problem only gradually (Meier, Wrinkle, and Polinard 1994).

In the bottom-line agency relationship, bureaucrats are technocrats. They are hired for their expertise and the organization is built around the goal shared with the principal. Unless the agent tries to shift the blame during periods of crisis, none of the common principal-agent problems occur. This pattern of relationships fits many government corporations, including federal deposit insurance, and perhaps antitrust policy under President Reagan (Wood and Anderson 1993). Bureaucracies dominate these policy areas by inertia and expertise (akin to the automatic control systems on an oil tanker) but when something goes wrong, politicians come to the bridge and yank on the tiller. They then go back to the party deck and wait to see if something happens.

Case 7. Policy Subsystem: Goal Consensus, Both Principal and Agent Share Information

In situations with goal consensus and shared information, the classic policy subsystem will develop. Bureaucrats will share goals with members of Congress, and discretion will be granted to the bureaucracy as a result of trust. Monitoring will occur as incident to the continual process of consulting.

The scenario in which there is goal consensus and both principal and agent have substantial information is the classic policy subsystem. Goals are shared with little challenge as long as all members of the subsystem can be kept reasonably happy. Such relationships require repeat game situations with principals and agents interacting over long periods of time. Principals need this long tenure to develop the expertise necessary to participate in the process as peers with the agents. As a result, this case rarely develops in relationships between the president and the bureaucracy, but is likely to develop in relationships between Congress and the bureaucracy; it applies to most agriculture agencies and their relationships with Congress (Meier, Wrinkle, and Polinard 1993). Some might refer to this situation as one of congressional dominance, but that misrepresents what are essentially symbiotic relationships between members of Congress and the career bureaucracy. The influence should be regarded more as reciprocal than dominant. Witness the persistence of the agricultural policy subsystem despite the dramatic decline in the number of members of Congress from agricultural districts (Browne 1988). In this situation, discretion will be granted to the bureaucracy as a result of trust between the two parties. Monitoring will occur as incident to the continual process of consulting. Other possible areas where case 7 might describe the political bureaucratic relationships are health research, agricultural research, and similar distributive policy areas.

Case 8. Plato's Republic: Goal Consensus, the Principal Has Information but the Agent Does Not

Situations with goal consensus where principals have information but agents do not are most likely to occur in polities with little administrative capacity. In such situations, the relationships between the principal and the agent will be similar to the relationship between the philosopher king and his/her serfs.

Cases like these are perceived to be rare in contemporary federal policy. Not all policy is made at the federal level, however. At local levels, bureaucracies rarely have the expertise and the administrative capacity that the federal bureaucracies do, so it is quite possible to have agents at the local level with an information disadvantage relative to principals. A city manager or a strong mayor governing a small city could be in this situation. It perhaps fits best the governing system in Plato's *Republic*. The republic had few laws with universal application; implementation problems were thus minimized and all citizens were expected to partici-pate actively in the city's political life. In such situations, principals should become expert philosopher kings; agents in such a situation could even be slaves.

This situation could well fit relationships that exist in small homoge-neous cities. Addressing such issues as nude dancing, parking meters on Main Street, low property taxes, dog licensing laws, etc., the principals are likely to have all the information necessary to make public policy. Agents, if there are any, have limited discretion and simply carry out the policies established by the principals. The only agency problem that might occur is shirking since goal consensus exists.

The Implications of This Model for Political Control

What are the implications of this model for political control of the bu-reaucracy? An obvious point is that we hypothesize that many different relationships can exist between principals and agents. This may not at first appear to be a startling finding, but when we peruse the bureaucratic literature, we find a tendency for scholars to adopt one model of bureau-cratic politics at a time, to the exclusion of all others. For example, at one time the politics-administration dichotomy was the ruling paradigm in the bureaucratic literature. Scholars then largely abandoned it in favor of the iron triangle and capture theories. Next, scholars moved to issue net-works and then adopted the principal-agent model.[3]

Our model suggests that such discrete theoretical thinking is simplis-tic. Different theoretical assumptions of the bureaucratic process are likely to hold simultaneously under different circumstances. For ex-ample, the basic conditions of the politics-administration dichotomy can exist if agents possess a great deal of information, their principals possess limited information, and goal conflict between the two sets of actors is limited. Similarly, however, the basic conditions of the subsystem or iron triangle model can exist if both principals and agents possess a great deal of information and goal consensus is high. Additionally, the conditions conducive to the principal-agent model can exist when agents have an information advantage and goal conflict is high. In short, the various discrete models that have for so long dominated the bureaucratic literature can coexist in a more generalizable model of the bureaucratic process.

To further demonstrate the lack of generalizability of models of political control of the bureaucracy, we need only to examine one of the model's basic assumptions; bureaucrats will actively employ their information advantages to shirk or avoid principal attempts at hierarchical control. This assumption means that agents must have an information advantage, a circumstance that exists in only two of the eight cases (cases 2 and 6). In the other six cases, either the principal has an information advantage over the agent (cases 4 and 8) or the agent and the principal have information (cases 1, 3, 5, and 7). Thus, of the eight possible cases in our model, only two conform to a key assumption of the principal-agent model. Moreover, we are somewhat skeptical of the notion that shirking is the major bureaucratic problem faced by politicians. Our assessment of the Reagan administration was that the politicians would have preferred the bureaucrats to shirk since the goal was to reduce the overall level of regulation. On the other hand, bureaucrats actually wanted to produce a larger number of outputs than their principals desired. Ironically, in this case, shirking could be interpreted as the desire of bureaucrats to produce a higher level of outputs.

When are attempts at political control of the bureaucracy most likely to occur? The assumption that agents actively employ their information advantages to shirk principal attempts at hierarchical control at least implies that agents exert some level of bureaucratic discretion. They must, almost by definition, have discretion in order to shirk. Furthermore, scholars (e.g., Lowi 1979) argue that bureaucratic discretion undermines attempts at overhead democracy. If there is such a direct connection between political control and bureaucratic discretion, then we also can ask, under which circumstances is bureaucratic discretion most likely to occur?

In four of the cases presented in figure 2.2, bureaucratic discretion should be severely limited. In cases 4 and 8, discretion is limited because the information asymmetry favors the principal. Consequently, principals can easily dominate the political relationship and limit bureaucratic discretion. In cases 1 and 5, both principals and agents have limited information and the role of the agent is hypothesized to be either a clerk or a cheerleader for the principal's policies; though as noted, in the case 5 situation bureaucrats do have discretion regarding how much they enforce the law (e.g., the analogy of the water faucet). Both cases suggest a largely passive bureaucracy with limited bureaucratic discretion. We can also further state that in cases 1 and 5 the need for political control is largely mitigated by the passive nature of the bureaucracy. Thus, bureaucratic discretion and the need for principal attempts at political control of the bureaucracy should not be problematical in the four cases presented on the left side of figure 2.2. In the four cases on the right side of figure 2.2, however, we hypothesize that agents are capable of exerting considerable, if varying, levels of bureaucratic discretion. Discretion, in large part, results from the agent's greater access to information. Thus, bureaucratic discretion should present its greatest threat to hierarchical control on the right side of figure 2.2 (cases 2, 3, 6, and 7). Does, however, the mere existence of bureaucratic discretion necessarily signify that agents will avoid political control? In cases 6 and 7 there is basic goal consensus between principals and agents. Goal consensus indicates an absence, or at least a severe limitation, of conflict. If there is general agreement on policy goals, then the need for political control of the bureaucracy should be greatly obviated. For example, what would be the purpose of a principal exerting precious political resources to control an agency that already agrees with the principal's basic policy objectives? Obviously, principals would have limited incentive to exert control, and agents would have a limited incentive to take policy in a direction that does not conform with either their own or their principal's basic goals. Consequently, the necessity of principal attempts at political control would be greatly obviated in any case in which goal consensus is high.

In short, political control of the bureaucracy should not be a problem when goal consensus is high (cases 5, 6, 7, and 8), when bureaucratic discretion is limited (cases 1, 4, 5, and 8), or when principals possess greater information than their agents (cases 4 and 8). Only two cases remain (cases 2 and 3) where political control of the bureaucracy should be actively contested on a regular basis. In these cases principals and agents are in conflict, bureaucratic discretion exists, and either principals and agents possess a great deal of information (case 3) or agents have an information asymmetry over their principals (case 2). We can further assert that of these two cases, the most problematical for political control of the bureaucracy should be case 2, because agents possess more information than their principals. Case 2, of course, is the traditional principal-agent model.

We can now ask another basic, but important question. Why, over the past decades, have bureaucratic scholars concentrated so much of their energy in an attempt to explain only one type of principal-agent relationship? The answer, from the above discussion, is that it is indeed the most problematical case for political control of the bureaucracy.[4] Agents possess both the greatest incentive and the greatest ability to avoid hierarchical control, much to the dismay of those who believe that the bureaucracy should work for them. In this sense, then, it is probably the most interesting case to explain.

Still, while case 2 situations may be interesting, a focus on any one of the eight possible political-bureaucratic relationships promotes a highly misleading normative conceptualization of bureaucratic politics. Because scholars have focused most of their attention on this one case, the image of the bureaucracy derived is one of a highly contentious, undemocratic relationship between recalcitrant agents and ill-informed principals. Clearly, figure 2.2 suggests that this is not a generalizable view of the entire realm of bureaucratic politics. In fact, if we look at figure 2.2 as a whole, we see that the bureaucratic process is much more consensual and much less confrontational than most scholarship presently admits. Political control by principals appears to be more the norm than the exception.

By concentrating on one of eight possible scenarios, we ignore much of what is pedestrian and mundane about bureaucratic politics, but nevertheless much that is important. Political-bureaucratic relationships are not always a cauldron of conflict. Bureaucratic politics is dynamic and conflict varies according to the level of information principals and agents possess and the level of goal conflict. By removing the assumption that information and goal conflict are constants, we already derive a radically different conceptualization of the bureaucratic process. As we contend in the next section, the traditional principal-agent model also incorporates other simplistic assumptions that greatly distort the reality of bureaucratic politics.

Multiple Principals

A point that will be empirically addressed later in this book is that the basic principal-agent model generally allows agents to have multiple principals but rules out any externalities. That is, principal A by hiring agent B does not infringe on the interests of principal C who also hires agent B. Relationships between political institutions and bureaucracy are interesting in part because the relationships do generate externalities. In a political system built around checks and balances, those same checks and balances show up in bureaucratic politics.

The more astute principal-agent studies allow for multiple principals (Moe 1985a; Wood and Waterman 1991, 1993, 1994; Scholz and Wei 1986; Krause 1999; also see Magat, Krupnick, and Harrington 1986). Congress, the courts, and the president are most frequently incorporated in principal-agent models, but if we relax the unrealistic notion that only elected officials seek to control the bureaucracy, the principal-agent logic can be extended to interest groups and other federal agencies (the Office of Management and Budget). Similarly, within an agency, an implementation-level bureaucrat could well have a principal-agent relationship with his/her superior, the head of the regional office, or the head of a state agency. With the introduction of the federal system (Wood 1992; Scholz and Wei 1986), the number of relationships multiplies rapidly.

If we permit the model to include multiple principals and allow that the relationship between principals and agents might be characterized by externalities, what are the implications for the study of bureaucracy? First, the existence of multiple principals strongly indicates that all principals will not agree on goals, and goal conflict among principals makes the relationship between principals and agents exceedingly complex. If the EPA cannot implement the goals of the Reagan administration without ignoring the goals of the Congress, then the logic of the principal-agent model breaks down. No matter how well the monitoring systems are designed and how well the principals structure the rewards and sanctions, one of the principals, and perhaps both, will be dissatisfied with the relationship.

From the perspective of the bureaucracy, the notion of conflicting policy goals is not unusual. The political process rarely resolves all the disputes that force an issue onto the political agenda; actors not satisfied with the macro political process are quite likely to continue to press their goals on the bureaucracy (Truman 1951; Freeman 1965; Rourke 1984). Bureaucracies are caught in a web of conflicting goals espoused by Congress, the president, federal courts, the media, the regulated industry, environmental groups, state government agencies, and other politicians at different levels of government.

One option for multiple principals would be to simply interpret all relationships as dyads that resemble principal-agent relationships. Such an interpretation clearly would be incomplete as a result of the externalities problem as well as the limited resources possessed by bureaucracies. With multiple and conflicting principals, bureaucracies have little choice but to act as political institutions and attempt to build some type of coalition-supporting policy. A bureau-centric approach (Hill 1991; Lowery 1993) would focus on the strategies and tactics of the bureaucracy as it seeks to establish a coherent policy. An alternative theoretical framework, advocacy coalitions, would treat the bureaucracy as one political actor among many (Sabatier and Jenkins-Smith 1993). The advocacy coalition framework, at its base, downplays the hierarchical relationships in a principal-agent model and examines the political relationships among various actors. Another alternative is that agents perceive and organize principals into various constituency-like groups based on similarities in the type of influence they perceive each principal as exerting. Again, the focus is on multiple and likely competing principal interactions with the bureaucracy.

The introduction of multiple principals with externalities is in many ways fatal for the classic principal-agent model. Although the model is built around voluntary transactions, it does have a normative element in that principals are supposed to control agents. With the introduction of multiple principals—many, if not all, with claims of political legitimacy—the principal-agent model offers no resolution about which principals should be responded to and which should be ignored. More importantly, unlike the bureaucratic politics or advocacy coalition approaches, it cannot predict actual bureaucratic behavior because it has no way of establishing any hierarchical relationships or even order among the various principals. From a strict principal-agent framework, then, bureaucratic behavior might appear random (or even as shirking), yet can easily be explained by the political goals and resources of various principals and the goals of the bureaucrats.

On another general level, the existence of multiple, competing principals, and quite likely multiple and competing agents, also means that the existence of a pure information asymmetry is less likely to occur. For example, if there were competing principals, then agents (even those with an information asymmetry) would have an incentive to ally themselves with principals who most closely reflect their basic policy goals. In those cases where principals do not share the agent's goals, bureaucrats would have a clear incentive to leak information to other competing principals who do share their objectives. While agents would likely still possess more information than any of their principals, the end result would be a breakdown of a pure information asymmetry.

The case of competing principals within an agency, or the presence of goal conflict within an agency, also has been ignored by the traditional principal-agent model. Yet, in some agencies, such as the Federal Trade Commission (FTC), the membership has to reflect both Democrats and Republicans. Since appointments are staggered over time, only two-term presidents are likely to be capable of appointing all of the members of an agency such as the FTC. Since appointees hire staff, reorganize units, set budgetary allocations, and so forth, the existence of competing principals within an agency can be quite important. Because agents within an agency also may not share the same goals (which could represent even a further elaboration of the idea of goal conflict presented in figure 2.2), the incentive for leaking and information sharing would likewise increase. Again, the existence of competing principals and agents within an agency has critically important implications for the principal-agent relationship. The tendency would be for the bureaucratic model to more approximate an advocacy coalition approach rather than a traditional principal-agent relationship.

Finally, when we add interest groups to the model, the likelihood that an information asymmetry will exist further diminishes. Interest groups, by definition, are interested in a particular policy area. Unless there is goal consensus between interest groups and bureaucrats, interest group members will have a clear incentive to take the information they derive to other political principals. The arsenal now available to interest groups is of course formidable, including the Freedom of Information Act, litigation, and other mechanisms designed to make information accessible to the public. The presence of interest groups as ongoing political actors again suggests that over time the most likely outcome is a case

3 scenario. In short, while case 2 situations may be the most theoretically interesting cases to study, in reality, they may occur with much less frequency than scholars have heretofore acknowledged.

Some Other General Limits of the Principal-Agent Model

Voluntary and Non-Voluntary Relationships

The principal-agent model was developed for relationships that are voluntary; a contract is a voluntary relationship entered into between a buyer and seller that is mutually advantageous to both participants. The model is a way to overcome some market flaws. Such a model is unlikely to fit government relationships smoothly for two reasons. In government, the relationships are not voluntary; they are mandatory. The president has to have a relationship with the EPA; there is no other game in town for environmental policy. Likewise, political principals cannot fire bureaucratic agents (the action of last resort in a principal-agent model). In a market system, some compliance is always possible because the patient can change doctors if the agent does not provide satisfactory service. Political principals, at least those with limited terms facing a career merit system, do not have this option. As a result, they are forced to rely on lesser controls and face a stronger possibility that their objectives will not be carried out.

Unidirectional Influence

The principal-agent model, as used in the political science literature, tends to portray relationships as unidirectional.[5] Clearly bureaucrats influence the behavior of principals (see Krause 1999). President Reagan would have had no reason to take action against the regulatory bureaucracies if they had not previously implemented policies that he did not like. Similarly, the EPA resisted Reagan's appointees with media leaks and appeals to Congress. The resulting support eventually caused a change in tactics on the part of the principal to a less confrontational approach. In agriculture, assessing the responsibility for major farm legislation is difficult because bureaucratic agents place many of the issues on the agenda; they regularly hold conferences before farm bills expire and provide a forum for alternative policy proposals. The exact language in legislation is frequently worked out between Congress and the agencies (Browne 1988; Browne et al., 1992).

The Unitary Actor Problem

The principal-agent model assumes a principal interacts with an agent. As applied to political science, these models generally assume implicitly if not explicitly that the actors are unitary. That is, the president is assumed to act as a single unitary actor, as is the bureaucracy. This is akin to the formal theory simplifications based on models with two legislators, one interest group, and one bureaucrat. The effort is to simplify in order to make the study more tractable.

The unitary actor assumption, however, violates a great deal of what we know about both political actors and bureaucrats. Students of bureaucracy have long rejected the unitary actor assumption (Simon 1947; Downs 1967). Bureaucracies are composed of individuals with a variety of interests that might not completely coincide with the goals of the organization.[6] Different professions within an organization might have different policy objectives (Eisner 1992; Kelman 1980). Central office staff might see policy differently from those in the regional office (Hunter and Waterman 1996). Implementation bureaucrats are often at odds with the policy formally promulgated by the agency hierarchy (Mazmanian and Sabatier 1983). Groups of career bureaucrats might even see a change in political leaders as an opportunity to reopen old bureaucratic disputes and gain the upper hand on their intra-agency rivals (Pfiffner 1988).

Political institutions also can be viewed as a set of coalitions rather than a single unitary actor. Presidential staff may have interests different from the president; the Office of Management and Budget might pursue a policy at odds with the president's stated intent. Congress, similarly, rarely speaks with a single voice. Individual committees often press distinctly different goals within a policy area. The different interests are well illustrated by the 1993–1994 health care debates with different committees providing forums for a variety of interests. Often principal-agent studies equate responsiveness to a committee with responsiveness to Congress (Mackay, Miller, and Yandle 1987) or simply assume that actions taken in the name of the president are in fact actually supported by the president. In the first case, what is presented is an incomplete view of the process. That the environmental committees have a principal-agent relationship with the EPA is correct, but so do the energy committees, and the small business committees, and none has a priority claim over the others; all must be considered principals. Similarly, the president is only one person; the institutionalized presidency is a bureaucracy with all the inherent principal-agent problems of a bureaucracy, that is, lower-level personnel may take actions that are not endorsed by the upper reaches of the hierarchy.

Reintroducing Dynamics into the System

Principal-agent models are supposed to be dynamic, not static. They characterize relationships that develop and evolve. We think the defining feature of the dynamics of political bureaucratic relationships is information. Political actors, whether politicians or bureaucrats, learn over time about both policy and politics; all institutions also develop some capacity over time. This change in the pattern of information has the potential to move a relationship from one cell of our base model to another. The introduction of information in some cases may even have the impact of changing goals as policies demonstrate that certain approaches are or are not effective. The dynamic contribution of information suggests why some policies evolve over time (those where information is valuable) and why other policies simply repeat past mistakes (those where information is discounted).

Simply arguing that the principal-agent model is a theoretical cul-de-sac is not enough. By arguing that information and goal conflict/consensus are not constants, but rather continuous variables in a bureaucratic model, we believe we have laid the basic groundwork for the development of a more generalizable theoretical framework. It is one that allows us to include the often mundane and perfunctory relationships that can and do exist between many principals and agents in bureaucratic settings. Yet it also acknowledges that the bureaucratic process can be highly political and even conflictual. We do not for a moment contend that our model is complete. Our acknowledgement that there can be goal conflict between agents within a single bureaucracy raises yet another possible modification of the model presented in figure 2.2. Still, as a starting point, we believe we have credibly argued that the bureaucratic process is far more complex, far more dynamic, and much more interesting than prior research has indicated. At the same time, the complexity and the dynamics can be clustered into a modest number of logically related cases to facilitate research.

In addition, the model presented in figure 2.2 has a certain symmetry to it that suggests a more generalizable model. To the left of the model, we anticipate that bureaucratic discretion generally will be limited, particularly as it relates to changes in policy. To the right, as the agents' access to information increases, discretion should likewise increase. To the bottom of the model, goal consensus indicates that there will likely be less conflict between principals and agents. At the top of the model, we argue that conflict over goals will be more intense. In cases 2 and 3, at the top and right of figure 2.2, bureaucratic discretion and goal conflict is combined, and so we further argue that political control of the bureaucracy will be more problematic in these situations.

Additionally, the top and bottom of the model have a symmetry that may not at first be obvious. For example, case 3 situations, involving high levels of information on the part of principals and agents, as well as high conflict, suggest a group dynamic—in this case advocacy coalitions. In the comparable situation without conflict, case 7, the group dynamic remains, but in this case it reflects a more consensual iron triangle relationship. Likewise, cases and 2 and 6 are symmetrical. Case 2, the traditional principal-agent model, is by far the most conflictual and the most political. Case 6, on the other hand, is the least conflictual and the least political. On the left side of the figure, cases 4 and 8 also exhibit a similar symmetry. In case 4, where principals possess a great deal of information and agents do not, and where goal conflict is present, agents are passive, acting largely as staff to principals. In case 8, given similar circumstances, but without goal conflict, agents are again passive, but this time operate more as willing slaves, since the conflict between principals and agents has been removed. In cases 1 and 5 principals and agents possess little information. When goal conflict exists (case 1), bureaucrats are again passive and clerical in nature. When goal conflict is removed (case 5) bureaucrats, while again largely passive in nature, now operate as cheerleaders, willingly promoting the principal's policies.

In addition to this symmetry, two final points need to be made about our model. First, while we have, for heuristic purposes, presented the eight cases in figure 2.2 as discrete situations, in reality we believe the model to be more continuous than discrete in nature. Agents never have all of the information and principals none of it. Clearly, this scenario is highly simplistic. A continuous formulation better captures the dynamics of the bureaucratic process. We believe, however, our fundamental point still holds. As the level of an agent's or principal's information either increases or decreases, and as the level of conflict either increases or decreases, we expect the political relationships between the two sets of actors to change, as well.

This point segues nicely into our final point. While we have presented eight cases, we do not mean to suggest that a relationship between a principal and an agent will always be characterized by the same case over time. For example, the relationship between principals and agents in the airline and motor carrier industries (the Civil Aeronautics Board and the Interstate Commerce Commission) was, for many years, best described as a case 7 situation. With the introduction of the deregulation issue in the 1970s, however, the situation quickly evolved into a case 3 situation (Waterman 1989). Understanding how the politics in these cases was altered is, we believe, one of the principal (no pun intended) strengths of our approach.

3

The Nature of
Bureaucratic Politics

Along with the principal-agent model, William Niskanen's (1971) model of the budget-maximizing bureaucrat is one of the most prominent theories of bureaucratic politics. It is similar to the principal-agent model in that it focuses on an "agency problem," or the idea that "the incentives of bureaucrats do not lead to behavior that is fully consistent with the interests of politicians" (Niskanen 1991, 15). Niskanen's theory posits that bureaucrats strive to maximize budgets. Thus, the behavior of bureaucrats can best be understood by assuming that the bureaucrat "is a 'chooser' and a 'maximizer' and, in contrast to his part in the characteristic method of sociology, not just a 'role player' in some larger social drama" (Niskanen 1994, 5). Unlike principal-agent models, Niskanen's theory is not only an explanation for bureaucratic behavior, but is designed to explain the existence of budget deficits. Because bureaucrats constantly seek to maximize their agency budgets, budgetary allocations increase and deficits result.

There are seven key elements to Niskanen's theory (1971, 1975, 1991, 1994; the citations in this and the next several paragraphs come from 1991, 16–17). First, "bureaucrats are much like officials in other organizations. Their behavior will differ, not because of different personal characteristics, but because of the incentives and constraints that are specific to bureaus." Niskanen then adds a caveat: "this assumption does not deny that bureaucrats may have different characteristics, nor would the theory be refuted by observed differences in these characteristics." For instance, he does not dispute the fact that bureaucrats are more likely to work in agencies where "rewards are more consistent with their own preferences." For Niskanen, however, the central issue is not the different characteristics of bureaucrats, but rather the difference between private firms and public organizations.

In this regard, the second element of Niskanen's theory is important because most "bureaus face a monopoly buyer of their service, usually some group of officials. The effective demand for the output of a bureau is that of this political sponsor, rather than that of the ultimate consumers of this service." Third, most "bureaus are monopoly suppliers of their service." Fourth, the "bilateral monopoly relation between a bureau and its sponsor involves the exchange of a promised output for a budget, rather than the sale of its output at a per-unit price." Fifth, as "in any bilateral monopoly, there is no unique budget output equilibrium between that preferred by the sponsor and that preferred by the bureau." In this process both the sponsor and the bureau have advantages. "The sponsor's primary advantages in this bargaining are its authority to replace the bureau's management team, to monitor the bureau, and to approve the bureau's budget. The bureau's primary advantage is that it has much better information about the costs of supplying the service than does the sponsor."

Thus, as with the principal-agent model, not only is there conflict over objectives between sponsors/principals and bureaus/agents, the agent also is assumed to have an information advantage. There are other similarities between the theoretical approaches. With regard to his sixth element, Niskanen continues, "The sponsor's role in this bilateral bargaining over budget-output combinations is further weakened or modified by two other conditions. The sequence of prior budget-output decisions provides relatively more information about the sponsor's effective demand for the bureau's service than about the cost of providing this service. In addition, the sponsor does not have sufficient incentive to monitor the bureau, because it shares only a small part of the benefits of more efficient performance by the bureau."

Hence, even in repeat game situations the principal does not reduce the information advantage the agent possesses nor is monitoring a costless option. As noted in chapter 2, monitoring is a key concept identified in principal-agent models to offset the information asymmetry problem. Niskanen argues, "efficiency monitoring is a public good among legislators and voters. This leads the sponsor to use its authority primarily to capture part of the bureau's surplus in ways that serve the specific interests of the sponsor group, rather than the interests of the broader group of legislators and voters."

Finally, the seventh element of Niskanen's theory is that "neither the members of the sponsor group nor the senior bureaucrats have a pecuniary share in any surplus generated by the bureau. The effect . . . is that the surplus will be spent in ways that indirectly serve the interests of the sponsor and the bureau, but not as direct compensation."

While Niskanen made some changes to his basic theory (for example, rather than arguing that sponsors are passive he later argued that they seek to maximize the political interests of the committee members [1991, 22–23]), these seven elements remain the key elements of his theory. As noted, in many respects they parallel the assumptions of the principal-agent model. Since both are economics-based models, this is not surprising.

Perhaps even more than the principal-agent model, Niskanen's theory has been widely referenced and employed in studies of bureaucratic politics. It also has been much criticized. Conybeare (1984) challenged Niskanen's assumption that bureaus will always produce an output greater than that of a private industry, thus promoting an efficiency loss. He found this to be true only if a bureau "can exercise perfect price discrimination in its relation with its financial sponsor." Likewise, other factors such as competition can reduce inefficiency.

On the other hand, Banks (1989) found that because of the information asymmetry, agents have considerable advantages over legislatures in the budgetary process. While legislatures can monitor or audit an agency's budget, they do so at considerable cost. Consequently, the legislature has an incentive to avoid auditing requests unless the benefits of doing so exceed the costs. Miller and Moe (1983) similarly find that agents have considerable advantages (including an information asymmetry) in their budgetary relations with the legislature.

According to Bendor, Taylor, and Van Gaalen (1985), however, the advantages of the information asymmetry can be mitigated. They argue that even imperfect monitoring can reduce the bureaucracy's tendency to maximize its budgets. As the probability of legislative detection increases, bureaucrats are less likely to overstate their budgetary requests.

Bendor, Taylor, and Van Gaalen (1987) also examine the possibility that bureaucrats may be uncertain about the about the behavior of their superiors (or sponsors), while Bendor and Moe (1985) present an adaptive model that includes participation by interest groups, bureaus and politicians. In this model, participants act adaptively rather than choosing to maximize their behavior, such as through a budget-maximizing strategy. Again, one conclusion to be drawn from these studies is that it is possible to mitigate the agent's information advantages.

Blais and Dion (1991, 6) also critique Niskanen's assumption of a budget-maximizing bureaucrat. They note that the theory has clear assumptions regarding the behavior of bureaucrats: "There is a formal model with strong assumptions: Budgets are the sole component in bureaucrats' utility function. Budget maximization is the only objective being pursued and all . . . strategies are geared toward that specific goal."

Yet, is budget-maximization the "only objective" of bureaucrats or are they motivated by other goals? Brehm and Gates (1999) find that bureaucrats in a variety of federal, state, and local agencies are motivated by "functional" and "solidary" goals; that is, they are motivated by the tasks they perform and by a desire to secure acceptance and respect from fellow employees. While pecuniary reward is important, it is not the primary motivating factor; nor is supervisor oversight. A number of other studies likewise raise questions about the motivations of bureaucrats and whether they act as budget-maximizers (see Blais and Dion 1991; Downs 1967). Later in this book we examine the budget-maximizing thesis by examining how much attention agency personnel pay to their budgets and how much knowledge they have about them.

Active or Passive Sponsors?

As previously mentioned, one of the key elements of Niskanen's original thesis, but one that has undergone some reinterpretation, is the idea that principals or sponsors are essentially passive. When Niskanen first formulated his theory in the early 1970s, most bureaucratic scholars agreed with his characterization of sponsors as largely passive. In other words, it was a widely shared scholarly perception that sponsors such as Congress (particularly the body as a whole rather than its individual committees), the president, and the courts were not interested in bureaucratic politics. In fact, the dominant theory of bureaucratic politics at the time—the capture or iron triangle theory—posited that sponsors such as the president, the Congress, and the courts played only a limited role in overseeing or controlling the bureaucracy. Thus, it was not unusual for Redford (1969, 48), in one of the classic works on the bureaucratic process, to argue: "The ability of overhead political institutions to prescribe is limited, not only by the complexities of interests pressing for continuous representation through established roles, but also by the complexities of organization itself."

Congressional and presidential scholars also promoted this idea. For instance, Scher (1960) believed that members of Congress were more interested in satisfying constituencies than they were in overseeing the bureaucracy and Harris (1965) argued that Congress had limited ability to control the bureaucracy. Dodd and Schott (1979, 173) also wrote, "The highly dispersed nature of oversight responsibility, the lack of strong central oversight committees, and the natural conflict among committees all undermine severely the ability of Congress to conduct serious, rational control of administration." Likewise, Lowi (1979, 307) commented, "Little in the political science literature is clearer than the analysis of Congress showing shortcomings of efforts to gain administrative accountability through legislative oversight and through the development of legislative intent." Even in the late 1980s, Bryner (1987, 74) wrote, "There are few incentives for members of Congress to invest much time in oversight of agency rule making and other activities."

Congress was not the only principal assumed to be a passive sponsor. Similar views were expressed about the presidency's ability to control the bureaucracy. As Ripley and Franklin (1986, 41) wrote, "governmental bureaucracies are not fully controlled by any superior. The structure of the Constitution—both written and unwritten—is such that they are free to bargain over their own preferences. They have some accountability to Congress and the president, but it is not final . . . This is not a fact to be unthinkably deplored or applauded. But it is a fact that is central to our understanding of the behavior of bureaucracy in the United States."

In his influential textbook, *The American Presidency*, Rossiter (1960, 19–22) asserted that the most difficult task presidents face is not trying to sell their programs to Congress, but rather to the bureaucracy. In another prominent presidential textbook, Koenig (1975, 184) stated that even more resistant than Congress "to the president's quest for dominion of the executive branch is the giant bureaucracy itself, with its layers of specialists, its massive paper work . . . lumbering pace, [and] addiction to routine." Similarly, Cronin (1980, 333) wrote, "The federal bureaucracy . . . is one of the most visible checks on a president." Noll went even further (1971, 36), stating, "Although the president could exercise authority . . . there is little evidence that he or his administration makes much of an attempt to do so." Other scholars (e.g., Yandle 1985; Cohen 1985) provided empirical evidence suggesting that the presidents and other principals were unsuccessful in their attempts to influence the policies of a number of federal regulatory agencies.[1]

Likewise, the courts were perceived as largely passive participants in the bureaucratic process. Woll (1963, 109–10) wrote that the "courts have retreated from exercising meaningful oversight." In short, while there were a few notable exceptions (e.g., Rourke 1984), most scholars agreed that principals were uninterested in or incapable of overseeing the bureaucracy. Yet if it could be shown that principals are interested in or are capable of controlling the bureaucracy, this would have important implications for Niskanen's budget-maximizing bureaucrat model. It would suggest that, at a minimum, imperfect monitoring actually can occur and that, as Bendor, Taylor, and Van Gaalen hypothesize (1985, 1987), bureaucrats' inflated budgetary requests would more likely be detected. As a result, agents would be more uncertain about their superiors' intentions. Likewise, the presence of active, multiple principals also could raise issues for the principal-agent model's assumptions of information asymmetry and goal conflict. What, then, is the empirical evidence with regard to principal or sponsor interest in overseeing the bureaucracy?

In the 1980s and 1990s, with the rise to prominence of the principal-agent model, scholars produced a series of economics-based mathematical models and quantitative studies demonstrating that political principals indeed can control the bureaucracy. For instance, Calvert, Moran, and Weingast (1987), Calvert, McCubbins, and Weingast (1989), Bendor, Taylor, and Van Gaalen (1985, 1987), and Ferejohn and Shipan (1989) examined the potential of legislative influence over the bureaucracy, while another, related literature examined the relative costs and advantages of control versus delegation (see Fiorina 1981; Kiewiet and McCubbins 1991; Epstein and O'Halloran 1994, 1996; Huber and Shipan 2000, 2002; Huber, Shipan, and Pfahler 2001) and hence why legislators would delegate authority to the bureaucracy in the first place. Aberbach (1990) found that congressional oversight was more prevalent than past scholars had assumed, while McCubbins and Schwartz (1984), using the analogies of police patrols versus fire alarms, argued that oversight did not have to be systematic in order for it to be effective.

As a new legislative political control literature flourished, Moe (1982, 1985a) and Stewart and Cromartie (1982) argued that the president also played a key role in the bureaucratic process. Both provided empirical evidence that presidents use their appointment power to influence the bureaucracy. Using qualitative methods (Nathan 1983; Waterman 1989) and empirical ones (Wood 1988, 1990; Wood and Waterman 1991, 1993, 1994; Waterman and Wood 1992, 1993) scholars provided consistent evidence that presidents either could control the bureaucracy or, at the very least, were not passive participants in the bureaucratic process. Moe (1985b) provided theoretical reasons for a larger presidential role in bureaucratic politics, while Moe (1985a) and Wood and Waterman (1993, 1994) also demonstrated that the courts can influence bureaucratic behavior.

In sum, beginning in the 1980s scholarly perceptions about the interaction between principals and their agents fundamentally changed. It is now widely assumed that political control of the bureaucracy is not only possible, but that it is even a two-way street, with principals influencing the behavior of their agents and agents influencing the behavior of their principals (Krause 1999). Scholars are even able to identify the specific mechanisms (e.g., appointments, budgets, reorganizations) that political principals use to influence their bureaucratic agents (see Nathan 1983; Waterman 1989; Wood and Waterman 1991; Carpenter 1996)

While scholarly perceptions regarding the nature of principal interest in bureaucratic politics changed, the focus to date has been on a rather small subset of political principals: usually the president, Congress, occasionally the courts, and even less often the public or public interest groups (though see Bendor and Moe 1985; Furlong 1998; Carpenter 2002). Our goal is to identify the importance of multiple principals and to present a more nuanced view of the bureaucrat's political world. To accomplish this objective, we will examine the perceptions of bureaucratic agents working in two environmental agencies (one federal and one state) and analyze their perceptions of the political principals with which they interact. We will examine bureaucratic perceptions of the president, the Congress and the courts, as well as different types of interest groups (environmental, business, and agricultural), various state and local officials (including governors, state legislatures, mayors and county officials), political appointees (the EPA administrator, the EPA regional administrators), and even the regulated industry (once a focal point of capture and iron triangle studies but generally overlooked in principal-agent research).

Our Methodology

We employed survey research methods to examine how bureaucratic agents perceive the influence exerted by a variety of political principals. Several studies have employed this method to analyze the bureaucracy, but only a few specifically for the purpose of examining the subject of political control (e.g., see Furlong 1998; Stehr 1997). For example, Heclo (1977), Kaufman (1981), Aberbach and Rockman (1976, 1990, 1995), Cole and Caputo (1979), Aberbach, Putnam, and Rockman (1981), Gormley (1987), and Brehm and Gates (1999) have examined the attitudes of bureaucrats in considerable detail, but not directly as part of the political control of bureaucracy literature.

To examine bureaucratic perceptions we used a structured survey instrument and examined two universes of environmental personnel. The first instrument was a survey of the employees of the Environmental Protection Agency's National Pollutant Discharge Elimination System program, which deals with the regulation of surface water under the Clean Water Act and its amendments. We focused on the perceptions of enforcement personnel because most of the top-down political control literature has examined their actions—such as inspections, notices of violation, and administrative orders—as dependent variables. We decided to examine the EPA because many top-down studies (see Wood 1988; Wood and Waterman 1991, 1993, 1994; Waterman and Wood 1993) already have provided extensive findings supporting the propensity of EPA bureaucrats to respond to cues for action by the principals (e.g., the president, the Congress, and the federal courts) We therefore expected to find similar evidence from a bottom-up study of EPA enforcement personnel. We also wanted to examine the perceptions of state-level bureaucrats. Therefore, the second survey examined the perceptions of employees of the New Mexico Environment Department. Responses for the EPA NPDES survey were collected between May and August of 1994. Survey responses for the NMED survey were collected between March and June of 1997. Although the surveys were not conducted at the same time, and thus some caution must be applied to any comparison, our intention was to examine how federal- and state-level environmental actors perceive the influence of various political actors.

The task of identifying EPA NPDES personnel was accomplished by obtaining organizational charts and telephone directories from each of the EPA's ten regional offices. Where possible, we also obtained lists of their NPDES personnel specifically. Two of the regional offices chose not to participate in the survey. Thus, our universe consisted of 189 enforcement personnel from eight of EPA's ten regional offices. For the NMED survey we examined all environmental personnel because the subset of individuals working in surface water programs was quite small. Our universe at the state level consisted of 462 employees. The only employees who were not surveyed were those with strictly clerical responsibilities.

Both surveys were administered through a mail questionnaire. This method has the advantages of eliminating interviewer bias, guaranteeing that all members of our sample would have an equal opportunity to be contacted, and providing the confidentiality necessary for agency personnel to answer questions of a potentially sensitive nature. One threat to validity when using a mail questionnaire is a low response rate. Because of the sensitive nature of our survey (i.e., we anticipated that many potential respondents would feel uncomfortable answering questions about their political superiors, as well as officials within their own agency) this point was judged to be of particular importance. To secure as high a response rate as possible we used the Total Design Method (Dillman 1978). With regard to the EPA survey we first sent an initial letter to all 189 members of our target group in which we identified ourselves and briefly described the nature of our survey. A week later we mailed a copy of the questionnaire with a cover letter and a self-addressed stamped envelope (SASE). Three weeks after that we mailed a second copy of the survey to those people who had not yet responded, along with another brief introductory letter and a SASE. Seventy-two surveys were collected from May 17 to August 31, 1994. Our response rate was 38 percent. For the second survey we mailed the cover letter along with the survey instrument on March 10, 1997 to 462 employees of the NMED. Then two weeks later on March 24th we mailed a second survey along with a second cover letter. We received 165 completed surveys. Thus, our response rate for this survey was 36 percent.

It is clear in both cases that a higher response rate would have obviated our concerns about a self-selection bias. We did thoroughly consider other alternatives such as a telephone survey. A telephone survey of bureaucratic elites, however, entailed several important threats to validity. First, our samples likely would have been biased toward those people who are most likely to be in the office at any given time. Since many EPA and NMED enforcement personnel are regularly in the field (e.g., those who do on-site inspections) this presented the possibility, as one state enforcement official told us, that we would end up interviewing "potted plants" rather than more active employees. Second, a telephone survey would have involved considerable institutional bias. We would have been interviewing employees in their offices where their responses could have been overheard by colleagues and supervisors. This was a particular concern since many EPA personnel (up to five in some regions) share the same phone. Since the nature of our survey involved some potentially sensitive questions, we were concerned that EPA and NMED personnel would be less willing to answer questions fully if their responses could be overheard. Third, various EPA and NMED officials, including several supervisors, were concerned that our survey would interfere with their office's daily operations. Since each interview would take approximately twenty minutes to complete, the administration of the survey could have been very disruptive. Finally, since we would have had to call back many employees, possibly leaving messages on answering machines or with another colleague or supervisor, we did not know what impact "the telephone tag bias" (as we call it) would have introduced. Hence, while a telephone survey initially seemed to be the best means of conducting the survey, we eventually rejected this option.

Demographic Data

Who are the respondents to our EPA NPDES survey? Forty-seven percent of the individuals who responded to the EPA survey were women, 53 percent were men. The average respondent worked at EPA for nearly nine and a half years, with the median length of service being seven years. Reflecting a large number of relatively recent arrivals, however, 37 percent had been at the agency for five years or less.

The survey of state bureaucrats at the NMED was not limited to technical personnel as was the survey of the EPA bureaucrats. Instead, all members of the NMED (except purely clerical staff) were given an equal chance to respond to the survey questionnaire. As a result, issues of comparability between the samples must be considered. Of the 158 (of 165) NMED respondents who listed their positions, 112 (71 percent) were in technical jobs directly related to enforcement, making them directly comparable the EPA sample. The other 46 (29 percent) were in managerial, administrative, or other support positions not included in the EPA sample.

Unlike the EPA sample, the NMED respondents were not evenly distributed by gender. Over three-quarters (78 percent) of the state members who responded to the survey were male. In addition, males held over 90 percent of the technical positions. The New Mexico employees also were asked about their racial/ethnic identities (unfortunately, this question was not asked of the federal EPA personnel). Of the 131 NMED members who participated, 65 percent (86 respondents) said they were white. Another 28 percent (36 respondents) listed themselves as Hispanic. The few remaining respondents were fairly evenly distributed between black (3 respondents), Native American (2 respondents), and Asian (2 respondents).

The average lengths of time individuals worked at the NMED was slightly shorter than their federal counterparts—seven years was the mean length of service, while the median was five years. This reflects a work force with less time on the job than the EPA group. At the NMED, 55 percent of all the respondents, and 60 percent of respondents in technical positions, had five years or less at the bureau, compared to 37 percent of those at the EPA.

Political Attitudes

Demographic data provide us with only a rudimentary sense of who is charged with protecting the environment. We also are interested in what these individuals think about politics and other issues

According to David Gergen (2000, 87–8), President Nixon "did not trust the hundreds of thousands of people who worked" in the bureaucracy. "He had checked, he told his cabinet in 1971, and found that 96 percent of civil servants were against the administration. 'They're bastards who are here to screw us,' he reportedly said."

While Richard Nixon's rants against the bureaucracy were particularly vitriolic, most presidents generally assume that bureaucrats are more liberal and more out of the political mainstream than the American public. Several studies have found that over time, the composition of the bureaucracy has become more ideologically conservative (e.g., Aberbach and Rockman 1976; Cole and Caputo 1979; Aberbach, Krauss, Muramatsu, and Rockman 1990; Aberbach, Rockman, and Copeland 1990; Aberbach and Rockman 1990, 1995). Since environmental protection is a proactive duty, that is, it requires active governmental intervention in the marketplace, we can assume that those people who protect the environment should be among the most liberal members of the bureaucracy. Therefore, our findings here, while only suggestive of bureaucrats in other agencies, should be considered as coming from an agency where liberalism (and support for governmental activism) would be most likely to occur. What then do they think about politics?

In order to determine the basic ideological leanings of EPA enforcement personnel, we asked respondents to identify their ideological beliefs on a seven-point Lickert scale ranging from very liberal to very conservative. We did so on two different dimensions: social and economic matters. As can be seen in table 3.1, on both questions the largest number of respondents put themselves precisely in the "middle of the road" (28 percent socially, 26 percent economically). Overall there was a slight tendency for the bureau members to place themselves on the liberal side of the social-ideology scale. On the other hand, we found the same tendency to place themselves on the conservative side of the economic-ideology scale.

The figures from the same time as the EPA survey (1994) regarding overall political attitudes for the general population show, at first impression, an even greater tendency toward centrism than did the EPA sample.[2] On the three-point scale, 45 percent of the general population considered themselves moderate, 31 percent conservative, and 18 percent identified their attitudes as liberal. Other sources confirm that this rank-order of preferences has been consistent since 1978, and that there has been little variation in their relative sizes since then (Ladd 1994). On a three-point scale it is reasonable to expect that the response of moderate will be chosen by some portion of those respondents who would label themselves slightly liberal or slightly conservative when provided with a seven-point scale. Similarly, someone who is liberal on economic matters but socially conservative could choose to describe their overall position

Table 3.1
Ideological Self-Placement on Political Issues: EPA and NMED

	EPA		NMED			
	Economic Issues	Social Issues	Economic Issues		Social Issues	
			All	Tech	All	Tech
Very liberal	6	4	3	5	9	10
Liberal	7	16	14	8	21	18
Slightly liberal	20	23	17	15	17	16
(All liberal categories combined)	**33**	**43**	**34**	**28**	**47**	**44**
Middle of the road	**26**	**29**	**19**	**20**	**20**	**21**
(All conservative categories combined)	**41**	**28**	**46**	**52**	**33**	**35**
Slightly conservative	17	1	26	32	16	17
Conservative	20	11	17	15	15	15
Very conservative	4	4	3	5	2	3

Notes: Figures given in rounded percentages of responses. Bold numbers show total percentage figures for middle of the road, combined liberal categories, and combined conservative categories.

as moderate. When the results of our survey are considered in such a light, it is easy to see the similarity between the responses of the bureaucrats and of the general public. The bias of the distributions in both cases is toward the center position. What is clear, however, is that the EPA respondents are not any more ideologically liberal than is the public at large.

Ideology is but one measure of political behavior. Another measure is partisan identification. Do EPA personnel mirror the public in their partisan identifications or are they more likely to be members of the Democratic Party? Over one-fifth (22 percent) of the EPA respondents declined to answer the question on partisanship, while of the 78 percent who did, another 30 percent (24 percent of the total) said they had no party preference. Therefore, 46 percent of the total number of respondents to the survey—just under half—claimed no party identification. This may reflect a general reluctance on the part of federal civil servants to seem too political, given that their jobs place formal limits on the amount of partisan activity in which they can engage. If so, then this does not suggest greater levels of partisanship among bureaucrats than the general public.

Table 3.2, however, shows that of the slightly more than half of our

Table 3.2
Political Party Identifications and Approval Ratings of EPA and NMED Employees

	EPA Party Identification			EPA Approval of Clinton's Performance	
	Total Sample N= 72	Total Responding to Question N= 56	Total of Dem. and Rep. Party Identifiers N= 39	Approve 67% N=45	Disapprove 33% N=22
Democratic	39	50	72	92	8
Republican	14	18	26	22	78
No party	24	30	N/A	63	27
Other party	1	2			

	NMED Party Identification		NMED Approval of Johnson's Performance		
	Total Sample N = 165	Total of Party Identifiers N = 121	Approve 14 % N=23	Disapprove 42% N = 68	Strongly Disapprove 44% N = 71
Democratic	46	62	8	43	49
Republican	23	31	27	41	32
Green party	5	7	0	50	50

Note: Figures given in rounded percentages of responses.

respondents who did specify a party preference, nearly three times as many identified themselves with the Democratic as with the Republican Party (39 percent and 14 percent, respectively, of the total). The party identifications (not to be confused with party registration) of the general populace the same year showed a near-even distribution of Democrats, Republicans, and independents—35, 31, and 34 percent, respectively.[3] Party preferences of comparably educated groups differ extensively between surveys, but none suggest a 3:1 ratio of Democrats to Republicans.

It is interesting to compare the overwhelmingly Democratic partisan identification of respondents with their social and economic ideological self-placements; very centrist overall and conservative on economic matters in particular. To reconcile these differences we cross-tabulated the results of the partisan identification and ideology measures (one at a time). We found that on the social-ideology scale, three Democrats identified themselves as slightly conservative, eight as middle of the road, and another seven as slightly liberal. Only nine identified themselves as liberal (seven) or very liberal (two). Hence, of the twenty-seven EPA bureaucrats who identified themselves as Democrats, 41 percent self-identified themselves as being on the middle of the road or the right (conservative) side of the social-ideology scale.

With regard to the economic-ideology scale, four bureaucrats identified themselves as slightly conservative, eleven as middle of the road, six as slightly liberal, four as liberal, and only two as very liberal. Thus, almost 56 percent of Democrats identified themselves as being either middle of the road or slightly conservative. While more bureaucrats in our survey identified themselves as Democrats than Republicans, the analysis of their ideological placement along two different scales provides little credence to the idea that they were predominantly liberal. In fact, on both scales, a large percentage (a majority on the economic scale) did not identify themselves as liberals at all.

Thus far, we have examined the political attitudes of EPA bureaucrats by examining their self-identified ideological placements and their partisan identifications. What about their attitudes on specific political questions? We asked our respondents, "In general, do you approve or disapprove of the job Bill Clinton is doing as president?" Sixty-seven percent of the sample said they approved, giving the president a considerably higher approval rating than he enjoyed from the public as a whole at the time. The approval rating, however, broke down very much along partisan lines: 92 percent of Democrats who responded said they approved, while 78 percent of responding Republicans said they disapproved of Clinton's job performance. Of those who approved of Clinton's job performance as president, 52 percent identified themselves in one of the three liberal categories, and nearly 32 percent in the middle of the road category. Interestingly, seven individuals (or about 16 percent) who identified themselves in one of the three conservative categories also approved of Clinton's job performance. Consequently, while liberals were, as one would expect, more likely to approve of the president, a fairly substantial percentage of non-liberals, 48 percent, also approved. This suggests a broader level of support for Clinton than he received from the general public, which was much more ideologically divided in evaluating his performance.

We also asked EPA bureaucrats if they approved of the job Bill Clinton was doing with regard to the environment. Here, support for Clinton was significantly lower: 54.5 percent approved of his performance, while 45.5 did not. Of those who approved of Clinton's environ-

mental policy, twelve identified themselves in one of the three liberal categories on the economic-ideology scale, ten as middle of the road, and
thirteen on the conservative end. With regard to the social-ideology
scale, seventeen who approved identified themselves on the liberal end
of the scale, ten as middle of the road, and eight on the conservative end.
Again, then, Clinton's approval rating on this aspect spanned the ideological scale. In summary, while Clinton's approval rating among EPA
bureaucrats was much higher than it was for the general public, it was
not simply the result of a liberal/Democratic bureaucracy falling behind
a Democratic president.

The evidence presented here suggests that EPA bureaucrats are more
likely to identify with the Democratic Party and to approve of a Democratic president than are the general public. Our results do not suggest,
however, that the EPA members are extremely liberal in any sense, which
is consistent with the other survey research on bureaucrats we cited earlier in this section.

In addition, the fact that relatively few of our EPA respondents
reported partisan preferences does not mean that they are politically apa-
thetic or non-participants in the political process. Only one of seventy-
two respondents said he/she was not registered to vote. An overwhelming 96 percent said that they voted in the 1992 presidential election (the
most recent prior to the survey), and 80 percent said they voted in their
state's most recent gubernatorial election. These data put the political
participation rate of EPA bureaucrats, as measured by voting behavior, far
above that of the general public, approximately 56 percent of whom cast
ballots in the 1992 presidential race. The EPA respondents also reported
voting at a higher rate than groups of comparable educational levels,
which, in the 1992 presidential election, was approximately 70 percent.

What of the NMED bureaucrats? NMED bureaucrats as a whole displayed a distribution of political ideology only slightly different from the
federal bureaucrats at the EPA. The results are displayed in comparison
to the federal sample in table 3.1. The patterns between the EPA and the
NMED were similar in that New Mexico bureaucrats also showed gravi-
tation toward the center, and tendencies to be more economically conservative while more socially liberal.

As was true of the EPA, the relatively large components of liberal
and conservative responses by the NMED personnel could be interpreted
as meaning that they are more ideologically polarized than is the popula-

tion as a whole. Still, as with the EPA sample, the modal distribution was toward the center of the ideological spectrum. Again, the responses of the NMED members do not warrant the conclusion that NMED bureaucrats are more liberal than is the general population.

The distribution for NMED technical personnel was even more skewed toward conservatism than was the sample as a whole. Fifty-two percent of technical personnel fell on the conservative side of the divide on economic issues, compared to only 41 percent of the EPA sample and 46 percent of the NMED as a whole. Thirty-five percent of state technical personnel said they were on the conservative side of social issues as well. Only 28 percent of EPA respondents and 33 percent of NMED respondents overall said this; these patterns show that state bureau members as a whole had preferences more like those of the EPA sample than did the technical respondents from NMED. The modal responses for NMED respondents were slightly conservative on economic matters and liberal on social matters, as opposed to the middle of the road response that was modal for EPA bureaucrats on both issue areas.

On the question of political party identification, the pattern displayed by state personnel as a whole was similar to that of the federal responses. Table 3.2 shows the results of the NMED members' partisan preferences. The responses none or no party were not offered to the NMED respondents, so the overall difference between the groups in the percentages who offered no partisan preference was wide—47 percent of the EPA versus 23 percent of the NMED personnel. Strictly speaking, the Democratic to Republican ratio is actually lower in the New Mexico sample than in the federal one—2:1 compared to nearly 3:1, respectively. This difference largely disappears when the Green Party in New Mexico is considered as a faction from the state's Democratic Party. The New Mexico Green Party's agenda would fit on the left side of the liberal-conservative divide, though it has attracted some disaffected Republicans in several political races. For the limited purpose of examining party identification in this case, it is reasonable to combine Democrats and Greens for analytical purposes into a "left" or "liberal" amalgam party. When this is done, a distribution of 69 to 31 percent emerges—nearly 3:1—which is much closer to the proportions reported in the federal EPA sample. As was noted above, this distribution of partisan identification is substantially biased toward the Democratic Party compared to the American population as a whole. The Democrat-Republican ratio for

New Mexico in 1997, in terms of party identification, was approximately 2:1. So, when compared to the general population of New Mexico, which is substantially more Democratic than is the nation as a whole, the NMED bureaucrats are still more likely to identify with the Democratic Party.

We also wanted to measure the political attitudes of NMED bureaucrats. We therefore asked state employees if they approved of the overall performance of their elected chief, Governor Gary Johnson (a Republican). Four responses were possible, ranging from strongly approve to strongly disapprove (while only two responses approve/disapprove were offered on the EPA survey). Here, quite a different picture emerged from the federal personnel's ratings of President Clinton. Nearly 86 percent of the NMED respondents said they either disapproved or strongly disapproved of Johnson's performance as governor. Three more respondents strongly disapproved than simply disapproved. Only twenty-three members (14 percent) said they approved, and none strongly approved of his job performance. Unlike the EPA bureaucrats' assessments of Clinton, the NMED personnel's opinions of Johnson (a Republican governor) did not divide so strongly along party lines. While 92 percent of Democrats disapproved or strongly disapproved of his performance, so did 73 percent of his fellow Republicans, and 44 percent of that group strongly disapproved. Some of the low approval ratings in this case may be due more to the fact that Johnson had a particularly poor relationship with the NMED as an agency than to overall ideological preferences among the employees.

To get at this point, we also asked NMED bureaucrats to rate Gary Johnson's performance in relationship to the environment. When we did, only 1 percent of NMED bureaucrats strongly approved of his performance, while 16 percent approved, 38 percent disapproved, and 45 percent strongly disapproved. Hence the governor's job approval rating on this aspect was actually slightly higher, with 17 percent approving (versus 14 percent overall), but essentially mirrored his overall rating. Again, both Democrats and Republicans found fault with the governor's job performance.

In sum, these results indicate that, like their EPA cohorts, NMED members are more Democratic in their party preferences than is the population generally. This does not translate, however, into an ideological disposition more liberal in total than that of undifferentiated society, or of groups with similar educational characteristics.

As for political participation, the New Mexico bureaucrats reported an even higher level of voter participation than did the EPA personnel. Fully 91 percent of those who responded to this question (148 out of 162 responding) said they had voted in the last presidential election, and almost as many, 88 percent (142 out of 161 responding), had voted in the last New Mexico governor's contest. Because the New Mexico survey was conducted in 1997, the presidential race to which they were responding (the question on both survey instruments specified the last presidential election) was that of 1996, rather than 1992 as was the case for the EPA members. Overall participation in the 1996 presidential race was even lower than in 1992, which probably makes the state respondents even more unusual than the federal group in their high rate of balloting, and far more prone to voting than any other subgroup of the population about whom records are reported.

Environmental Attitudes

Thus far we have examined only the political attitudes of federal- and state-level bureaucrats. Other attitudes are relevant, as well. As Brehm and Gates (1993, 1999) note, bureaucrats in a variety of local, state, and federal agencies are motivated by "functional" and "solidary" considerations, that is, rewards deriving from the job itself. Consequently, the environmental attitudes of EPA and NMED personnel are of considerable relevance.

Most obvious are their attitudes with regard to the environment itself. It is not unreasonable to argue that bureaucrats involved in the business of environmental protection should be strongly committed to the goal of enforcement and, further, that they should be likely to rank problems addressed by their offices as more important than other issues. Hence, while we did not find bureaucrats at the state or federal level to be political extremists, they may still be what some critics of the agency (e.g., conservative and business groups) call environmental extremists. To examine this point we turn next to an analysis of the environmental attitudes of EPA and NMED bureaucrats.

Because our respondents are charged specifically with enforcing environmental laws, it stands to reason that their attitudes about environmental issues might influence their enforcement approaches. We asked our EPA respondents several questions about their attitudes toward and perceptions of environmental issues. A logical starting point was to find out how severe they thought environmental problems were at present (for EPA, 1994). Therefore, we asked them to what extent they agreed or disagreed with this statement: "The environment can be made clean and safe without making drastic changes to our lifestyle." We assumed that respondents who perceived the problems facing the environment to be more serious would be more likely to say that lifestyles needed drastic modification. Yet, a majority of our respondents (57 percent) agreed with the statement that drastic changes in lifestyle *were not necessary* to make the environment clean and safe. Those who indicated a strong reaction to this statement, however, were nearly equally divided between strong agreement (14 percent) and strong disagreement (15 percent). Clearly, this is not evidence of environmental extremism.

Stronger evidence of a commitment to the environment, though, can be found in the personal behavior of EPA bureaucrats. Eighty-three percent of our respondents indicated that they would be willing to keep their home thermostats at sixty-five degrees Fahrenheit during the winter. Nearly all (95 percent) indicated that they would be willing to take alternative transportation to work if it was made available. In fact, almost 78 percent said they already commuted to work by means other than driving their own cars; over half of our NPDES respondents indicated that they walked, bicycled, or took public transportation to work, and 25 percent carpooled. While a majority of EPA bureaucrats believe drastic changes were not required to make the environment safer, most were willing (or already were practicing) activities in their personal life designed to promote a cleaner environment.

We also wanted to know how EPA bureaucrats evaluated the environment in relation to other issues. As we noted, we expected them to consider the environment as the most pressing problem. Yet, when enforcers were asked what they thought was the single most important issue facing America today, only 10 percent indicated the environment. This ranked environmental issues in a tie for fourth place, well behind crime (first) and education (second) as national concerns, and slightly behind the economy (third). If it is reasonable to expect that environmental issues would have high salience for NPDES personnel, then this result is somewhat surprising. Certainly, it does not lead to the conclusion that these bureaucrats are environmental zealots. In addition, 10 percent of our respondents eschewed our list and offered their own most important issues, which included "moral decay," "population problems," and "political corruption." From the same list of issues, we then asked our respondents to rank the second through sixth most important issues. Ten percent ranked the environment as the most pressing problem, 16 percent second, 27 percent third 29 percent fourth, 14 percent fifth, and 4 percent sixth. The environment was ranked as either the third or fourth most pressing issue facing America by over half of the EPA NPDES personnel who responded to this question.

Enforcement personnel also were asked which area of environmental law enforcement they thought deserved the most attention in the United States. The greatest number (24 percent) said that water pollution should be the primary target of environmental enforcement. Because all of these officials worked in surface-water pollution control, it is interesting that 76 percent of our respondents said that something other than water pollution should be the top priority: 17 percent chose air pollution, and 16 percent hazardous waste disposal. Twenty-one percent of our respondents said multimedia cases should be the top priority of environmental enforcement, while 11 percent identified land management, 4 percent energy, 3 percent solid waste, and 4 percent simply said "other."

All in all, these results suggest that the NPDES personnel charged with administering the law are by no means "fanatics" about environmental problems generally, nor do they have a particularly biased assessment of the severity of water pollution problems as compared to other environmental issues. Unfortunately, we were not able to ask the same questions regarding the environment of the NMED personnel, largely due to survey space and cost considerations. We did, however, ask NMED personnel, "Is the environment an economic or a social issue?" To this question, 46 percent identified the environment as a social issue, while 54 percent identified it as an economic issue. Again, these results do not suggest that NMED officials were any more zealous in their view of the environment than were the EPA personnel we surveyed. In fact, the picture that emerges from both the EPA and the NMED is that their bureaucrats cannot be described as "zealots" in Downs's (1967) sense of the word. Rather, the environment was but one of many issues with which environmental personnel were concerned.

Our examination of personnel from the EPA and the NMED are consistent with a growing body of scholarly literature and shows that bureaucrats are less liberal and even more moderate than they are popularly portrayed. Additionally, the evidence with regard to attitudes about the environment indicates that they are not zealots. Thus, the often-popularly reported portrayal of the bureaucrat as a liberal "zealot" is not borne out by the results of either of our surveys. Finally, our analysis shows a remarkable degree of congruity between the views of federal- and state-level bureaucrats. While some differences do emerge, the overall picture is one of similarity and not differences.

4

An Examination of the Assumptions of the Principal-Agent Model

Past research has examined the possibility that the politics of federal regulatory agencies, such as the EPA, and state regulatory agencies, such as the NMED, should conform to the assumptions of the principal-agent model (see Moe 1982, 1985a; Scholz and Wei 1986; Brudney and Hebert 1987; Wood 1988; Hedge, Scicchitano, and Metz 1991; Hedge and Scicchitano 1994; Wood and Waterman 1991, 1993, 1994; Waterman and Wood 1993). In chapter 2, we also argued that federal regulatory bodies are the most likely agencies to conform to the assumptions of the principal-agent model. Given these assumptions, we expect to find evidence of an information asymmetry favoring the agent, and goal conflict between principals and agents when we examine the perceptions of EPA and NMED bureaucrats.

An Information Asymmetry

What are the conditions under which an information asymmetry is most likely to occur? First, one can hypothesize that the greater the level of expertise involved in an agency's functions, the harder it will be for principals to monitor a bureaucracy's behavior, and the more likely it will be that an information asymmetry exists (see Waterman and Gill 2002). As noted in chapter 2, the more information the bureaucracy has, the more likely it also is to have discretion; therefore political control issues are likely to be more prevalent, assuming that goal conflict also is present. Consequently, evidence of expertise is a reasonable precondition for the existence of an information asymmetry. If considerable discretion also is present then agents have both of the tools that would be necessary to avert overhead political control. The assumptions of the principal-agent model then would best conform to an agency that has expertise, discretion, and goal conflict with its principal(s).

Expertise

One measure of expertise is the quality of the training that bureaucratic personnel possess. The more technical the level of training, the more difficult it should be for a principal to monitor and therefore control an agent's behavior. A surrogate for expertise is the number and type of degrees held by EPA and NMED personnel. For both surveys we excluded clerical workers and examined only those individuals who actually enforce environmental laws or, in the case of the NMED, those with management responsibilities. In the case of the EPA we only surveyed enforcement personnel working for the NPDES program. The data on the level of expertise and training for EPA NPDES personnel are presented at the top of table 4.1.

Fifty-five individuals from the NPDES responded to this question. When asked to list their degrees and the field in which they were awarded, a total of seventy-six undergraduate and graduate degrees were reported; fifty-three respondents had bachelor's degrees and eighteen had at least one postgraduate degree. Only seven respondents stated that they did not have any degrees. Almost 53 percent (or twenty-eight respondents) who had BA and BS degrees had received them in engineering disciplines—19 percent each in chemical and civil engineering. Another 19 percent were from biology. In total, 89 percent of the undergraduate degrees held by respondents were in engineering or the physical sciences.

Of the eighteen individuals with postgraduate degrees, only two respondents completed master's degrees in civil or chemical engineering. All but one MS (no MAs were reported) were in engineering or a physical science other than biology (seventeen of eighteen or 94 percent). There is evidence, then, that the EPA NPDES respondents hold highly techni-

Table 4.1
Distribution of Total Degrees Awarded: EPA and NMED

EPA	BA/BS	MS	Other	Total (%)*
Biology	10	0	0	10 (13)
Chemistry	4	0	0	4 (5)
Other physical science	5	5	0	10 (13)
Chemical engineering	10	1	0	11 (14)
Civil engineering	10	1	0	11 (14)
Environmental engineering	3	6	0	9 (12)
Other engineering	5	4	0	9 (12)
Other fields	6	1	5	12 (16)
Total (%)*	53 (70)	18 (24)	5 (7)	76 (100)*
NMED	Bachelor's BA/BS	Master's MA/MS/MBA	Other (Doctorates)	Total (%)*
Physical science	94	35	8 (5)	137 (65)
Engineering	18	5	4 (2)	27 (13)
Social science / humanities	14	2	7 (4)	23 (11)
Business / finance	3	3	10	16 (8)
Other / unspecified.	2	1	4	7 (3)
Total (%)*	131 (62)	46 (22)	33 (16)	210 (100)*

*Percentages rounded. May not equal 100.

cally oriented degrees, most in scientific areas directly relevant to the enforcement tasks they perform.

What about the NMED bureaucrats? Again, as noted above, clerical workers were excluded from the survey. Still, the 143 NMED respondents who responded to the question about their level of education represent a more diverse group in terms of educational achievement and background than the much more specialized EPA NPDES response set. Like their federal counterparts, however, the NMED members were a highly educated group. As seen at the bottom of table 4.1, the technical employees at NMED were in fact slightly more educated than their EPA counterparts; 38 percent of the NMED technical personnel had postgraduate degrees, compared to 31 percent of the EPA respondents. The 143 NMED respondents held a total of 210 degrees: 188 at the bachelor's level or above, and 57 graduate-level degrees (master's, doctorates, and JDs).

Unlike the federal sample, which was dominated by engineering degrees (52 percent) only 13 percent of the state employees' degrees were in engineering fields. Nearly two-thirds (65 percent) of the NMED members' degrees were in physical sciences, as compared to 31 percent of the EPA respondents. The most highly represented physical science disciplines among the NMED sample were geology, biology, and environmental science, comprising 37 percent (or fifty-one) of the physical science degrees, and 24 percent of all degrees held. Social science and humanities degrees, barely represented in the EPA group, accounted for 11 percent of the degrees held by NMED personnel.

In sum, both groups were highly educated and held a large percentage of specialized degrees, mostly in engineering and the physical sciences. The fact that so many EPA and NMED bureaucrats held similar types of degrees suggests that training in these fields is of great value and importance to personnel in carrying out their enforcement tasks. This suggests a high level of specialized knowledge or expertise—precisely the kind of information that would make an information asymmetry more likely to exist.

The Exercise of Discretion and Bureaucratic Outputs

As noted, a high level of discretion also is likely in situations where agents take advantage of an information asymmetry. Unfortunately, on this point we only have data for the EPA bureaucrats.

For a highly technical agency, some measure—and often a considerable amount—of bureaucratic discretion is required in order for agents to perform their jobs.[1] This is so because while agencies face technical complexity, most laws cannot be written with such specificity that they identify the proper course of action for each and every possible situation a bureaucrat might face. This is particularly true when bureaucrats deal with highly technical issues requiring expertise that the principal does not possess. In these cases, bureaucracies are created and bureaucrats are given the discretion to perform tasks that legislators and their staff may not even fully understand. While the level of discretion delegated to the bureaucracy by hierarchical political actors is likely to vary according to prevailing political conditions, such as whether it is a period of united or divided government, as well as a particular agency's structure (see Epstein and O'Halloran 1994, 1996, 1999; Volden 2002; Whitford 2002), some measure of discretion is expected to exist in a federal regulatory agency such as the EPA.[2] In fact, as Bryner (1987, 207) writes: "The EPA's statutes are much more detailed than those of their sister agencies, but with only a few exceptions, such as those for automobile emissions under the Clean Air Act, the agency is given little guidance about the substance of regulations. . . . The statutory responsibilities dwarf the resources given, and give little guidance for how they should be allocated. EPA statutes include lengthy lists of actions to take and deadlines to achieve that the agency cannot even begin to accomplish. This does little to set priorities or give direction: if everything is a priority then nothing is."

As Hunter and Waterman (1996) note, environmental enforcement also is made more difficult to constrain because the source of pollution is not easily identifiable, particularly with regard to water pollution (the purview of the NPDES program). Hence, even if the law is written in what appears to be a clear and concise manner, with goals, priorities, and methods of enforcement clearly identified, in practice, bureaucrats will face situations for which the law does not provide clear guidance. Thus, enforcement personnel are likely to perceive themselves as having some level of discretion to implement the law.

Also, as our pre-survey conversations with various individuals in the EPA Water Office, as well as our examination of various enforcement documents (including the EPA's Enforcement Management System manual) indicated, the actual work of the NPDES enforcement personnel is incredibly varied. Some employees work within the water departments of their regional offices, while others work in enforcement departments. Some inspectors visit only agricultural sites, others visit chemical plants or public utilities, and still others are responsible for clients of every type of permittee (that is, NPDES permit holder, or the regulated industry) in their area. In states with primacy (that is states that have primary authority to enforce the Clean Water Acts—about four-fifths of the states had primacy in 1994), the enforcement personnel might deal mostly with the environmental department of that state rather than directly with permittees. In some regions, NPDES personnel are responsible for enforcement systems that reflect the priorities of the regional directors, while in other regions, priorities are heavily influenced by each of the different states within that region. At the same time, the EPA administrator and officials in the Washington central office also attempt to influence enforcement policy. Thus, EPA personnel respond to a wide array of policy actors, both inside and outside of their agency.

Given this remarkably diverse regulatory environment Ringquist (1995a, 36; see also 1995b) notes in his study of the EPA Office of Water

Quality, "Public bureaucracies play a legitimate role in American government not simply by responding to political directives, but also by using their expertise to craft policy solutions. . . . Government would be almost impossible if agencies did not sometimes act on these larger perspectives of responsiveness and legitimacy." Thus, there are a number of reasons why we should expect EPA NPDES personnel to have discretion.[3]

On the other hand, the behavior of an individual in any organization is constrained by rules and norms of that organization. Standard operating procedures (SOPs) and other rules are in place to guide the bureaucrat in decision making. There is oversight by direct and indirect superiors, feedback from supervisors and coworkers, and incentives and sanctions in place to make sure that the rules are followed (see Wilson 1989). Still, the institutional decision-making context can be classified by the amount of expertise and information available, the tractability of the issue, or its relationship to the knowledge possessed by the outside political sphere (see Gormley 1986). Under these criteria, we would expect to find evidence of discretion in EPA NPDES enforcement.

To get at this issue, we measured bureaucratic discretion by asking EPA bureaucrats which task they perform, how often they perform it on a monthly basis, and "how much personal discretion" they perceive themselves as having when they perform five different compliance and enforcement tasks: permit reviews; inspections; issuance of warning letters; notices of violation; and administrative orders. These activities were chosen because they represent a variety of enforcement actions where one might expect variation in both outputs and perceived discretion, depending upon the severity of the enforcement action.[4] Permit reviews are a monitoring mechanism when changes are made to an NPDES permit or at regular intervals when the current permit expires. Inspections also are characterized as a monitoring function and generally occur every one to two years. Warning letters or notices of violation are compliance actions. They are sent to violators of the NPDES program when evidence arises that a permittee is not in compliance; warning letters are the less severe of the two enforcement options. An administrative order is also a high-level compliance action. It can include a fine as well as a schedule for compliance. It is the last step in the enforcement process before civil action (criminal action is rare) is begun against a violator of the NPDES permit system. Based on our interviews, our analysis of EPA documents, and past work by Hunter and Waterman (1992, 1996), we expect greater levels of discretion to be associated with inspections than with permit reviews, since the rules for inspections are more clearly delineated. Also, we would expect lower levels of discretion as we move from warning Letters, to notices of violation, and finally to administrative orders.

Of these enforcement actions, which and how many do EPA NPDES enforcement personnel perform? As shown in table 4.2, 90 percent of the EPA enforcement personnel we surveyed were responsible for recommending the issuance of administrative orders. The next most widespread responsibility was sending warning letters (68 percent), and performing inspections (60 percent). Slightly more than half the respondents (57 percent) also issued notices of violation and conducted permit reviews (56 percent).

In the lower part of table 4.2 we list the number of enforcement tasks (1–5) in which each person could be involved to get a measure of how many people perform multiple enforcement tasks. We found that

Table 4.2
Enforcement Activities Performed by NPDES Personnel (N = 72)

Compliance or Enforcement Activity	Number of Respondents who Perform Activity (%)				
Permit review	40 (56%)				
Inspection	43 (60%)				
Warning letter	48 (68%)				
Notice of violation	41 (57%)				
Administrative order	65 (90%)				
Number of areas	1	2	3	4	5
Number of people involved	7	12	20	18	15

Table 4.3
Monitoring and Enforcement Actions (per respondent per month)

Activity Performed	Total Number Performed (% of all activities)	Mean Number Performed	Standard Deviation	Modal Number (% in Category)
Permit review	238.5 (34.8%)	6.3	8.8	1.0 (32%)
Inspection	89.8 (13.1%)	2.1	2.4	1.0 (51%)
Total monitoring	47.9%			
Warning letter	191.5 (27.9%)	4.2	5.9	1.0 (30%)
Notice of violation	109.4 (16.0%)	2.8	2.9	0.0 (23%)
Administrative order	56.4 (8.2%)	0.9	1.1	0.5 (15%)
Total enforcement	52.1%			
Total	685.6 (100.0%)			

about half as many people are involved with one aspect of NPDES (e.g., inspections) as they are with all five aspects, with a plurality responsible for three areas of compliance/enforcement. This finding suggests that there are very few specialists among the respondents and that most of them deal with a broad range of the NPDES enforcement process. Still how often does each task factor in to their total amount of work?

Table 4.3 lists the mean numbers of monitoring and enforcement actions performed, standard deviations, and the modal category for each action. Of the 685.6 mean number of enforcement actions per month reported by the survey respondents, almost 35 percent (238.5) were permit reviews. Combined with inspections, the monitoring activities account for 47.9 percent of all enforcement actions. The two monitoring activities are similar in that they are both required on a periodic basis and can be triggered in response to noncompliant behaviors. Permit reviews and inspections are therefore routinized, and the discretion involved in their performance may be subject to more administrative and legal boundaries than the other tasks in this study.

The enforcement behaviors, however, are always in response to noncompliance. Within this group, higher-level actions, such as administrative orders (56.4 per month, or 8.2 percent of all actions), are the least performed task. Administrative orders are employed less frequently than warning letters, the lowest (or least severe) level enforcement option of the three options given.

We next asked the EPA NPDES bureaucrats how much discretion they thought they had to deal with each of these five monitoring or compliance tasks. The results for perceptions of discretion questions for four of the five activities (inspections, warning Letters, notice of violations, and administrative orders) are presented in table 4.4. We asked a somewhat different question to get at the level of discretion in the permit review process, because of the different nature of that task, so the responses to that question are not presented in this table.

For each type of task, a plurality perceives themselves as having some or a great deal of discretion. As expected, the activity for which the greatest number of enforcers stated they had complete discretion was the issuance of warning letters (15 percent). Unexpectedly, however, the issuance of notices of violation is the task over which the largest number of respondents said they had no discretion. Most EPA NPDES enforcement personnel therefore see themselves as having either "some" or "a

Table 4.4
Frequency Distributions: Perceptions of Discretion in Agents' Tasks

Variable	None	Very Little	Some	A Great Deal	Complete	N = (%)
Inspection	1 (2.3%)	4 (9.3%)	20 (46.5%)	17 (39.5%)	1 (2.3%)	43 (100%)
Warning letter	3 (6.4%)	3 (6.4%)	13 (27.7%)	21 (44.7%)	7 (14.9%)	47 (100%)
Notice of violation	3 (7.5%)	4 (10.0%)	16 (40.0%)	13 (32.5%)	4 (10.0%)	40 (100%)
Administrative order	1 (1.5%)	4 (6.22%)	28 (43.1%)	28 (43.1%)	4 (6.2%)	65 (100%)

great deal" of discretion. Furthermore, despite our expectations there was no clear pattern to these perceptions; that is, they were not related to the severity of the enforcement task.

As noted, for permit reviews we asked a slightly different question: "On a scale from 1 to 5, where 1 is minor adjustments and 5 is fundamental changes, in general, how would you characterize the changes you make or recommend in the permits you review?" The results to this question suggested lower levels of discretion than with the other four task assignments. Of the forty individuals who do permit reviews, 72.5 percent rated their discretion as a 1 or a 2, at the low end of the discretion scale. Furthermore, no one identified himself or herself as having the authority to make fundamental changes in the permit review process, and only 7.4 percent ranked their discretion level as a four on the five-point scale.

Still, the combined evidence indicates that EPA NPDES enforcement personnel do perceive themselves as exerting "some" or a "great deal" of discretion across four of the five monitoring/compliance tasks. While there are some variations from task to task, particularly with regard to permit reviews, most bureaucrats identify themselves as having discretion.

To better understand the causes of this discretion, we examined another factor that may lead to variations in enforcement and perceptions of discretion: the permittees, or regulated industry, that NPDES personnel regulate. We asked our respondents: "With how many permittees do you personally interact?" Responses ranged from zero to three hundred.

Eighteen percent of EPA personnel said they dealt with ten permittees or less, while about 39 percent identified themselves as dealing with twenty permittees or less. About 10 percent of the EPA enforcement personnel identified themselves as dealing with one hundred or more permittees.

One can hypothesize that the more permittees one deals with, the more discretion an enforcement officer would have, because one would have less time to dedicate to each permittee and hence would have to have greater flexibility in terms of dealing with each permittee. Yet, despite this expectation, we found no relationship between the number of permittees and perceptions of discretion.

The type of permittee that EPA bureaucrats oversee might also be related to the level of enforcement and perceptions of discretion. In our survey we asked EPA personnel to identify the type of permittee they dealt with most often. Nineteen, or about 27 percent, said they dealt primarily with industry, while twenty-four, or about 34 percent, dealt with sewage treatment facilities and only one, or about 1.5 percent, with agriculture. Twenty-six, or about 37 percent, said they dealt with another type of permittee or with multiple permittee types. Since past research shows that EPA personnel consider sewage treatment facilities to be among the worst polluters (see Hunter and Waterman 1996), we expected to find higher levels of enforcement activity dedicated to this type of permittee. We also expected to see higher levels of perceived discretion with regard to sewage treatment facilities than with other types of permittees because, again, greater flexibility may be required in the enforcement assignment. What did we find?

Industry was subject to permit reviews more commonly than sewage treatment facilities. About 60 percent of permit reviews conducted on industry or sewage treatment facilities monitored industry. With regard to inspections, the same number occurred among those who identified themselves as dealing primarily with industry and sewage treatment facilities. As we noted before, permit reviews and inspections are mandated by law and thus must occur periodically. Consequently, we expected less variation in these measures than in the other enforcement mechanisms. On the other hand, if sewage treatment facilities are a more problematic type of permittee, then we would expect to see a higher number of sanctions (e.g., warning letters, notices of violation, and administrative orders) issued against them. In fact, about twice as many warning letters were sent to sewage treatment plants than to industrial permittees. About three times as many notices of violation were issued to sewage treatment plants and, of the administrative orders issued to industry and sewage treatment facilities, 60 percent were issued to treatment plants. In sum, the type of permittee does have an impact on the number of enforcement actions issued, but does it have an impact on perceptions of discretion?

We found no evidence that the type of permit (industry or sewage treatment facilities only) is related to perceptions of discretion. In each case, the chi-square statistic fell far short of statistical significance. In short, EPA personnel perceive the same level of discretion whether they deal with industry or sewage treatment facilities.

Impediments to Enforcement

Thus far we have examined what EPA enforcement personnel do and how much discretion they perceive themselves as having. Factors that should limit discretion include impediments to enforcement or factors that presumably would constrain bureaucratic behavior. In our survey we asked, "The following are potential obstacles you may face when enforcing the law. Please rank the top five problems you most frequently encounter." Respondents were then given the following options: insufficient resource allocations, an inability to identify the source of the pollution, insufficient support from the courts, insufficient support from the federal government, insufficient support from the state governments, and bureaucratic inefficiency. Of these, the problem most commonly identified was insufficient resource allocations. About 47 percent, or thirty of the respondents, identified this as the number one problem. Another 28 percent, or fifteen of the respondents, identified it as the number two problem. Thus, about three-quarters of the EPA bureaucrats responding identified insufficient resources as the number one or two obstacle they face in enforcing the law.

The second most common impediment to enforcement was bureaucratic inefficiency. Twenty-five percent or sixteen respondents identified it as the number one problem, with an additional 30 percent, or sixteen respondents, identifying it as the number two problem.[5] Thus, about half of the respondents identified bureaucratic inefficiency as the number one or two obstacles to enforcement.

Relatively few people identified an inability to identify the source of pollution—a problem related to the difficultly of the regulatory task—as the number one (6.3 percent) or two (3.8 percent) problem. The other three categories involve impediments to enforcement caused by other players in the regulatory process. Of these, the state governments were considered to be slightly more of a problem (ranked number one by 6.3 percent) than the federal government (ranked number one by 4.7 percent). Few, however, only 1.6 percent, considered the courts to be an impediment to enforcement. When it came to identifying the second most common potential obstacle, 13.2 percent identified the state governments, 9.4 percent the federal government, and 7.5 percent the courts.

What do these results tell us? First, the greatest obstacles to enforcement are resources and bureaucratic inefficiency. The two are related. One involves funding from outside sources, while the other involves how efficiently resources are expended by agency personnel. Clearly, EPA bureaucrats do not perceive either funding as adequate or the expenditure of funds as particularly efficient. Hence, a large percentage of agency personnel lay the blame, resource-wise, both outside and inside their own agency.

This finding is particularly interesting. While we might have hypothesized that agency personnel would blame outside actors for a lack of sufficient funding, which would be consistent with the Niskanen (1971) budget-maximizing bureaucrat model, we would not have expected the same personnel to identify internal inefficiency as a problem. In fact, according to the Niskanen model, internal inefficiency is to be expected since bureaucrats, interested in maximizing budgets, will try to maximize slack resources, even if it means spending money inefficiently so that they can demand more money in the next budget cycle. Our analysis, however, shows that EPA bureaucrats perceive bureaucratic inefficiency as a problem.

On the other hand, the nature of the regulatory task (i.e., identifying the actual source of the pollution) is seen as a much less of a problem. More surprising to us is the low ranking of the three external political actors. We expected a higher percentage of respondents to identify the courts as an impediment to enforcement; yet in fact the courts ranked last. The EPA has been involved in a number of high profile legal actions (Melnick 1983) that have delayed implementation of the Clean Air Act of 1970. Yet our respondents did not see the courts as an obstacle to enforcement. Likewise, given the intergovernmental dimension of environmental enforcement, and the many problems of coordination involved in

it, we expected a larger number of individuals to identify state governments as an impediment to enforcement. Finally, given the frequency
with which politicians and the press bash the federal government, we certainly expected a greater frequency of responses in this category, as well.
What the EPA bureaucrats are saying, however, is that beyond the allocation of resources, they do not perceive other actors as impediments to
how they enforce the law.

Summarizing These Results

What do these results tell us about an information asymmetry? First, as
noted above, the high level of training and expertise should be related to
the existence of an information asymmetry, and high levels of discretion
should provide agents with the potential to take advantage of it. While
we can only report on perceptions of discretion here, which of course
can be different from actual discretion, it is clear that most EPA NPDES
personnel see themselves as having discretion across four of five different
monitoring/compliance tasks. The fact that this discretion was not related to the number or type of permittee an individual NPDES official
regulates suggests that discretion is not merely driven by the complexity
of the task. Rather, it is a widely shared characteristic of most EPA
NPDES employees.

With regard to impediments to enforcement or factors that should
limit discretion, agents most often identified inadequate resources and
bureaucratic inefficiency. They did not, however, identify political principals as an impediment to enforcement. We can extrapolate a bit here and
suggest that the identification of political principals rather than resources
would have been more convincing evidence of a hierarchical attempt to
constrain bureaucratic discretion.

Consequently, there is evidence that the conditions exist for an information asymmetry between principals and their EPA and NMED agents,
and that agents have the discretion to take advantage of it. This is consistent with past research and one of the key assumptions of the principal-
agent model.

Goal Conflict

The second key assumption of the principal-agent model (as identified in
chapter 2) is that goal conflict exists between principals and their agents.

Is there evidence that goal conflict exists between EPA or NMED bureaucrats and their political principals? Since EPA officials perceived inadequate resources and bureaucratic inefficiency as the most tangible impediments to regulation, goal conflict may arise when principals exert their budgetary authority.

The EPA and its Principals

Research demonstrates that the budget is a powerful source of presidential and congressional control of the bureaucracy (Wood and Waterman 1991, 1993, 1994; though see Wildavsky 1964 for a more incremental political perspective). While much past research therefore indicates that the budget is an effective tool of bureaucratic control, we do not know if any particular institution (the president or Congress) is seen as exerting a greater level of influence in relationship to this political control device. To find out, we asked EPA bureaucrats three questions. First they were given the following statement: "The way the EPA enforces the law now affects how much money the congressional appropriations committee will recommend for the EPA budget in the future." They were then asked if they strongly agreed, agreed, disagreed, or strongly disagreed with this statement. The same statement and response sets were then repeated for "the Clinton administration" and "the Office of Management and Budget," or OMB, the organization within the Executive Office of the President that sets the budgetary allocations for each agency (see Heclo 1975; Tomkin 1998). The OMB is one of the most feared agencies of government because of the role it plays in constraining bureaucratic funding.

The responses to the three statements suggest that EPA bureaucrats did not differentiate greatly between the congressional appropriations committees, an incumbent president, and his major organizational tool for influencing the budget. Rather, all were seen as about equally likely to recommend changes in the EPA budget on the basis of the way the agency enforces the law. Sixty-nine EPA officials responded to the statement about Congress, seventy to the statement about the Clinton administration, and sixty-eight to the statement about the OMB. About twice as many EPA bureaucrats strongly agree with the statement regarding Congress than with those regarding the Clinton administration or the OMB. Still, the relative percentages in this category are small: 8.7 percent for Congress, 4.3 percent for the Clinton administration, and 4.4 percent for the OMB. The only other difference is in the disagree category. Forty percent disagreed that the way the EPA enforces the law now has an impact on the Clinton administration's budget recommendation. This compares to only 34.8 percent who disagreed with the statement about Congress and 33.8 percent who disagreed with the statement about the OMB. Yet, beyond this difference the overall picture that emerges is of similarity regarding the three principals.

Another more direct way of getting at the issue of whether goal conflict exists is to ask about the commitment of the Congress or the president to environmental regulation. Presumably, the more committed they are, the more likely they will be to support the agency's mission, and the lower the level of goal conflict will be. To measure the commitment of the oversight actors EPA officials were asked, "How would you describe the Clinton administration's attitude toward environmental regulation?" They were then asked the same question with regard to the congressional oversight committees. EPA officials were given five options: very resistant, somewhat resistant, neither resistant nor supportive, somewhat supportive, and very supportive.

It is important to remember that the survey was conducted in 1994, before the Republican Party's takeover of Congress. This means that the Democratic Party, a party that is generally considered to be more pro-environmental than the Republicans, controlled both houses of Congress. Yet, while only 7 percent found the committees to be very resistant to environmental regulation, another 35.1 percent found them to be somewhat resistant. Thus, 42.1 percent of the fifty-seven EPA NPDES officials who responded to this question ranked the congressional committees in one of the two resistant categories. On the other hand, only 24.6 percent ranked the committees in the somewhat or very supportive categories.

Nearly a majority of EPA enforcement personnel (48.6 percent), however, classified the Clinton administration as somewhat supportive, while another 41.4 percent classified the administration as neither resistant nor supportive. None identified the Clinton administration as very resistant to environmental regulation and only a small percentage (4.3 percent) identified it as somewhat resistant. Clearly, then, EPA officials perceived the Congress to be less committed to environmental regulation than the Clinton administration; this is evidence of a higher level of goal conflict between EPA NPDES enforcement personnel and Congress than with the Clinton administration. The number of EPA bureaucrats who were willing to respond to these two questions provides further evidence. Almost everyone responded to the Clinton question (seventy out of seventy-two), while fifteen bureaucrats refused to respond to the congressional appropriations committee question.

This latter finding suggests that in terms of perceptions of goal conflict, in 1994, EPA NPDES enforcement personnel perceived greater goal conflict with (a Democratic) Congress than with (a Democratic) president. Is there evidence of the same dynamic with regard to state-level bureaucrats?

The NMED and its Principals

At the state level, the governor (in 1997, Republican Gary Johnson) and the state legislature (in 1997, controlled by a majority of Democrats) are the NMED's immediate hierarchical masters. We therefore asked NMED bureaucrats, "How would you describe the Johnson administration's attitude toward environmental regulation?" We asked the same question about the state legislature.

Of the 162 NMED respondents, 43.2 percent identified Governor Gary Johnson as being very resistant to environmental regulation. Another 35.2 percent identified him as being somewhat resistant. This means that overall, 78.4 percent found him to be resistant. On the contrary, only 6.9 percent found the state legislature to be very resistant to environmental regulation, with another 23.9 percent identifying it as somewhat resistant. Thus, only 30.8 or less than one-third found the state legislature to be resistant, while over three-quarters found the governor to be so. In fact, the modal category for the state legislature was somewhat supportive, with 36.5 percent of respondents describing it as such. As noted above, EPA bureaucrats believed that the Congress was far more resistant to environmental regulation than the president. Yet, perceptions were reversed when we focused on the state-level government in New Mexico.

To derive another measure of the governor's commitment to environmental regulation, we asked, "Since Gary Johnson's inauguration in January 1995, do you think the NM Environment Department has been more active in environmental enforcement?" Only 5 percent of the 161 NMED bureaucrats who responded answered yes to this question. When we asked the same question of EPA NPDES water enforcement personnel, however, 17.4 percent of the 69 respondents believed that the EPA had been more active since Clinton's inauguration in January 1993. The results here suggest that while neither the governor nor the president was seen as setting trends toward more active environmental regulation, the governor of New Mexico was perceived as much more resistant to regulation than the president.

Theoretical Implications

Thus far we have found evidence for the assumptions of the principal-agent model: an information asymmetry, the discretion to take advantage of the asymmetry, and goal conflict. Yet we also found that EPA bureaucrats were less likely to perceive goal conflict with the Clinton administration, while NMED bureaucrats were less likely to perceive goal conflict with New Mexico's state legislature. In other words, goal conflict does not necessarily exist equally between agents and each of their principals. Since our results suggest lower levels of goal conflict between the EPA and the Clinton administration, it would be logical for EPA bureaucrats to have aligned themselves with administration officials in conflicts with Congress, since the administration better reflected a commitment to the agency's goals. In the case of New Mexico, NMED officials would have had an incentive to align themselves with the state legislature. In fact, unstructured interviews with various environmental officials in New Mexico suggest that this is precisely what happened; bureaucrats dissatisfied with the Johnson administration actively reached out to allies in the state legislature to block unwanted gubernatorial initiatives.

Once we add two principals to the principal-agent model, what are the implications? According to Wood and Waterman (1994, 147), "The presence of multiple democratic principals violates the administrative precepts of hierarchy and unity of command. Competition between the president and Congress for power over the bureaucracy means that signals to the bureaucracy are often ambiguous. Communications are garbled, and the bureaucracy does not know which manifestation of influence to respond to."

Another possibility is that where different levels of goal conflict exist between agents and multiple principals, agents will have an incentive to strategically align themselves with a principal who best represents their interests, so long as that principal is perceived as having influence. Furthermore, once we extend this logic beyond the case of an executive and a legislature, the political game should be even more dynamic, with agents gravitating toward those sets of principals who best represent their interests. In other words, as was argued in chapter 2, in such cases, the resulting dynamic may be better represented over time by an advocacy coalition approach rather than the traditional principal-agent model. Once agents begin to build coalitions, they have incentives to share information with supporters/principals; thus mitigating the monitoring problem, at least to some extent. In addition, other types of principals (e.g., interest groups) could bring additional information to the bargaining table that may impact the political dynamic.

Yet, when scholars have written about multiple principals they have brought very little empirical data to the table. We therefore do not know how prevalent multiple principals are and how much influence bureaucrats perceive them as having. Again, various bureaucratic theories give us different clues as to what to expect. The capture/iron triangle/policy subsystem models suggest an insular relationship between an agency, congressional committee members, and the regulated industry, but posit little influence or even interest from outside sponsors such as the president or the courts. Empirical studies, many using the principal-agent framework, find that principals such as the president, Congress, and the courts influence or control various state and federal bureaucracies, but the focus is on a relatively small subset of political principals. The issue network and advocacy coalition literatures posit the potential for a greater number of principals, but even here the empirical evidence is sparse (though see Jenkins-Smith, St. Clair, and Woods 1991; Sabatier and Jenkins-Smith 1993). A more detailed empirical analysis of the prevalence of the influence of multiple principals is needed.

NMED Contacts with Multiple Principals

Bureaucrats deal with more than just the legislative and executive branches, though to what extent they deal with other policy actors is not clear. We know that they also deal with interest groups (both pro-business and pro-environmental), the public, the media, various state and local politicians, and the courts. It is therefore important to move beyond a narrow consideration of just a few political actors and toward an examination of the bureaucrat's broader political world.

Specifically, we wanted to know with which political actors bureaucrats interact, how often they interact with them, and how they interact with them. We therefore asked our NMED respondents the following questions: "In an average month, how many times does someone representing the following institution contact you personally? If they do contact you, please indicate whether the nature of the call is usually a specific question, a request for information, a request for action, or a complaint." The results are presented in table 4.5. The total number of contacts with political principals is reported in the first column. Subsequent columns then indicate the type of contact. Since principals can contact a bureaucratic agent in multiple ways, the summation of the types of contacts generally exceeds the number of reported contacts.

Obviously, since we are dealing with state bureaucrats, we did not expect, nor did we find, many contacts with the federal executive and legislative branches. Looking at the first column of table 4.5, we find that only one contact was reported with the president and thirteen with Congress. As for the governor, only eight contacts were reported, while twenty-eight contacts with the state legislature were reported. With re-

Table 4.5
Reported Contacts by NMED Bureaucrats with Various Political Principals

	Total #	Specific Question	Request for Information	Request for Action	Complaint
President	1	0	0	0	0
Congress	13	5	6	4	1
Federal courts	1	0	0	1	0
NM courts	8	3	3	1	1
NM governor	8	0	4	4	2
NM legislature	28	12	14	10	4
NM Department of Finance and Administration	10	7	2	2	0
NM Legislative Finance Committee	6	3	3	1	0
Environmental groups	67	31	42	19	14
Business groups	69	35	43	20	10
Agricultural groups	14	3	8	2	3
EPA administrator	28	19	12	12	2
Region six administrator	29	27	13	7	2
Media	55	23	39	1	1
Public	57	26	21	15	25
Mayors	24	13	10	7	2
County commissioners	25	7	13	9	5

gard to the Department of Finance and Administration (DFA), an institutional arm of the governor's office, only ten contacts were reported. Only six contacts were reported with the Legislative Finance Committee (LFC) of the state legislature.

In comparison, sixty-nine contacts were reported with business groups, sixty-seven with environmental groups, fifty-seven with the public, and fifty-five with the media. Twenty-nine contacts with the EPA regional administrator were reported, twenty-eight with the EPA administrator, twenty-five with county commissioners, twenty-four with mayors, and fourteen with agricultural groups. Few contacts were reported for either state (eight) or federal (one) courts.

The figures from the first column of table 4.5 indicate that, at least with regard to the frequency of contacts with principals, NMED environmental bureaucrats deal with a wide array of actors, many of whom are not executive or legislative branch officials. In columns two through five of table 4.5 we examine why bureaucrats were contacted. For this purpose, asking questions and requesting information are considered as lower-level interactions, while requests for action or complaints are higher-level interactions.

The two primary reasons for contacts appear to be to ask a specific question or to request information. Most of the business and environmental group contacts were for these two purposes. Almost all of the media's contacts were for these purposes. In terms of requests for action, the largest number are reported from business groups (twenty) and environmental groups (nineteen), though the public (fifteen), the EPA administrator (twelve), the state legislature (ten), the county commissioners (nine), and both the mayors and region six EPA administrator (seven) made a number of requests for action. As for complaints, the largest numbers are from the public (twenty-five), with environmental groups second at fourteen, and business groups third at ten. Only a few other principals were identified as having contacted NMED bureaucrats to express a complaint (county commissioners five times, mayors four, and the state legislature four times).

The results from table 4.5 indicate that NMED officials deal quite often with interest groups. While the capture and iron triangle theories incorporate interest groups as an integral part of their models, the principal-agent model has made little attempt to include them. It is apparent here that bureaucrats also deal quite often with the public and the media, which are also not included in most formulations of the principal-agent model. Consequently, it appears that principal-agent models, as presently framed, overlook some actors that actually play important roles in bureaucratic contacts.

In table 4.6 we next examine the method by which contact was made. We asked respondents to consider the seventeen principals, and whether any actors "have tried to influence your office in the past twelve months. Please indicate the most likely means (up to three) used by each participant." The options given were personal letters or faxes, telephone calls, personal visits, indirect contact via a supervisor, legal directives, or indirect contact via a legislator. We expected that bureaucrats would be more attentive to legal directives and to indirect contacts via a supervisor or a legislator than they will be to phone calls or letters/faxes. While a

Table 4.6
How Contact Was Made by Principals with NMED Bureaucrats

	Letter or Fax	Telephone Call	Personal Visit	Indirectly via Supervisor	Legal Directive	Indirectly via Legislator
President	1	0	0	3	10	7
Congress	11	8	0	10	23	14
Federal courts	0	0	0	3	37	4
NM courts	0	0	1	5	34	7
NM governor	13	9	2	73	26	26
NM legislature	20	21	8	30	20	26
NM Department of Finance and Administration	12	12	4	32	14	20
NM Legislative Finance Committee	10	11	5	30	15	26
Environmental groups	44	52	38	8	12	16
Business groups	91	48	38	32	7	31
Agricultural groups	13	18	10	13	3	16
EPA administrator	26	18	12	32	22	6
Region six administrator	25	25	17	33	21	3
Media	13	69	28	14	0	2
Public	46	64	43	17	2	15
Mayors	25	32	9	18	1	12
County commissioners	23	34	15	18	1	12

personal visit represents a mid level of contact, a legal directive or inter-cession via a supervisor or legislator is likely to get a bureaucrat's atten-tion and get it fast.

As is evident in the table, bureaucrats reported being contacted in a wide variety of different ways by each of the seventeen principals. The governor most often used intercession by a supervisor to contact NMED bureaucrats. The governor also was reported to have considerable con-tacts via legal directives and indirectly via legislators. Likewise, while state legislators were more likely to use letters/faxes and phone calls than was the governor, they also made the most of their contacts through legal directives and indirectly via either a supervisor or another legislator. The governor's DFA and the state legislature's LFC also were reported to have made most of their contacts indirectly via a supervisor or legislator or via legal directive. Business groups and agricultural groups also used the entire panoply of techniques to interact with NMED bureaucrats, including a large number of intercessions by legisla-tors on their behalf.

When the courts interact with NMED bureaucrats, they do so mostly via legal directives. Both the EPA administrator and the regional administrator for region six were reported to use all of the techniques to contact NMED officials, turning most frequently to contact via a supervi-sor and legal directives. Finally, the president and Congress, though they made few contacts, primarily used legal directives and intercession by a legislator.

While the governor, state legislature, DFA, LFC, business groups, the courts, and EPA and regional administrators used higher-level means of contacting NMED bureaucrats, other principals relied mostly on lower level contact mechanisms. For instance, environmental groups pre-dominantly contacted NMED officials via letters and faxes, phone calls, and personal visits, though they did sometimes use higher-level tech-niques. While the public was reported to use a wide variety of means to contact bureaucrats, they relied mostly on letters/faxes, phone calls, and personal visits. Likewise, the media most often used phone calls and per-sonal visits. The same was true of mayors and county commissioners, though they also used some indirect contacts via a supervisor.

These results indicate that the number of contacts is not the only im-portant criterion in examining the potential influence of political princi-pals. When we examine how contacts are made, we derive a clearer sense of how bureaucratic politics works. In particular, the results from table 4.6 demonstrate why the governor and state legislature are at the heart of the state-level principal-agent model. While relatively few contacts were reported, it is clear from the data that these principals were more likely to use higher-level contact mechanisms than were the media or the public, which made more overall contacts but relied more often on lower-level contact methods. Likewise, the results suggest that business and agricultural groups use higher-level techniques more often (as a percentage of all of their contacts) than do environmental groups. We can extrapolate from these results, and argue that NMED bureaucrats will be more likely to respond to those principals who use high-level contact mechanisms.

Overt Political Influence of EPA and NMED Bureaucrats

There is yet another way principals attempt to influence their agents: through overt political means. To examine this type of influence, we asked EPA and NMED bureaucrats: "In approximately how many, out of each ten cases that you personally deal with, would you say that overt political influence plays a role?" We then asked a follow-up question: "What sources outside of the EPA [or outside of the NMED] would be most likely to attempt to influence you?"

For EPA bureaucrats, a total of forty-seven (out of seventy-two) reported some level of overt political influence, ranging from one-half case in ten to ten cases in ten. The mode is one, with twenty bureaucrats reporting one case of overt political influence in ten cases. Twelve bureaucrats also reported that overt influence was used in two of ten cases. While this is not inconsequential, for NMED bureaucrats the pervasiveness of perceived overt political influence is considerably higher. One hundred four NMED bureaucrats (out of one hundred sixty-five) reported some level of overt influence. The mode again was one (with thirty reporting one in ten cases). Nineteen bureaucrats reported overt influence in two of ten cases, thirteen in three of ten cases, six in four of ten cases, fourteen in five of ten cases, eight in seven of ten cases, and eleven in ten of ten cases.

Who attempts to influence EPA and NMED bureaucrats? EPA officials identified a number of principals as having participated in overt political influence. Among them, twelve identified permit holders or the regulated industry, twelve Congress, eleven environmental groups, nine state-level EPA personnel, and four the public. As for NMED bureaucrats, at least one case of overt political influence was reported for each of the following principals: agricultural groups, "any attorney," business/industry, business action committees, the NMED bureau chief and division director, building contractors, the governor, the governor's staff, citizens' groups, city managers, county commissioners, the U.S. Congress, the U.S. Department of Energy (DOE), DOE contractors, members of the Democratic Party, the New Mexico DFA, the U.S. Department of Defense, environmental groups and activists, the EPA, federal regulators, "forest guardians," those receiving grants and loans, individual entrepreneurs, the lieutenant governor, mayors, the media, advocates of mental health for adolescents, "mining company spin doctors," the New Mexico Oil and Gas Association, petroleum marketers, PhD students at the University of New Mexico, private liquid waste installers, private water utility companies, the public, public opinion, the regulated community, state courts, state representatives, and state senators (that is, the state legislature). In other words, when we examine this list, we find that there are a large number of potential principals who attempt to directly influence the bureaucracy. This is further evidence that bureaucrats interact on a daily basis with a large and varied number of principals. It also suggests that when we model the principals who attempt to control or influence the bureaucracy we need to greatly expand the individuals and groups that we consider.

The Influence of Political Principals

In addition to contacts with bureaucrats, we also wanted to measure how much influence NMED bureaucrats perceive various political principals as exerting over how their office enforces the law. We asked NMED personnel about this issue; the scale was set from 0 to 4, from "no influence" to "a great deal of influence." In table 4.7 we present the results.

We have noted that the governor and state legislature made most of their contacts with NMED personnel through high-level mechanisms. Here we find that these actors are considered to be quite influential. The governor was ranked as the most influential principal and the state legislature second. In both cases, the influence of these actors was ranked higher than their main budgetary institutions (the state legislature's LFC

Table 4.7
NMED Personnel Rank the Influence of 17 Political Actors

Principal	Rank	Mean	Standard Deviation
1. NM governor	1	2.84	1.24
2. NM legislature	2	2.62	1.20
3. U.S. EPA administrator	3	2.27	1.29
4. U.S. Congress	4	2.11	1.45
5. NM Legislative Finance Committee	5	2.03	1.42
6. Region six administrator	6	1.00	1.35
7. NM Department of Finance and Administration	7	1.95	1.42
8. Public opinion	8	1.90	1.17
9. Business groups	9	1.82	1.33
10. State courts	10	1.81	1.25
11. Federal courts	11	1.78	1.29
12. Environmental groups	12	1.71	1.14
13. Media	13	1.55	1.08
14. President	14	1.43	1.45
15. County commissioners	15	1.20	1.21
16. Mayors	16	1.14	1.00
17. Agricultural groups	17	1.09	1.02

ranked fifth and the governor's DFA ranked seventh). The other state level actor, the state courts, was ranked relatively low (tenth overall).

Surprisingly, the U.S. Congress ranked fourth, while the president was ranked quite low at fourteenth. Business groups made greater use of higher-level contact mechanisms than did environmental groups. While business groups are ranked higher (ninth with a mean of 1.82) their perceived influence is roughly comparable to that of environmental groups (ranked twelfth with a mean of 1.71). Agricultural groups are ranked as the least influential principal.

Public opinion, while expressed most often through lower-level contacts, was ranked eighth with a mean of 1.90, not far below that of the DFA's influence, which had a mean of 1.95. This suggests that NMED bureaucrats do pay a great deal of attention to the public. They perceive the media as having much less influence, however. The media ranked only thirteenth and its mean influence, at 1.55, was much closer to the least influential principal (agricultural groups at 1.09) than to the most (the governor at 2.84). Likewise, the federal courts were ranked eleventh by NMED personnel, with a mean comparable to the state courts' influence (1.78 for the federal to 1.81 for the state courts). Finally, neither the mayors nor county commissioners were seen as exerting a great deal of influence.

These results show that NMED personnel perceive a wide variety of federal and state-level principals as exerting at least some influence. What, however, of the EPA bureaucrats we surveyed? To measure perceptions of influence, EPA enforcement personnel were asked, on a scale of 1 (no influence) to 5 (a great deal of influence) "How much influence do different institutions or individuals exert over your office?" EPA personnel were asked to evaluate fourteen different political actors with which they interact, including two types of presidential appointees: the EPA administrator and the ten regional administrators. The EPA rankings are presented in table 4.8.

The fourteen political actors are ranked by the mean or average amount of influence EPA personnel perceived them as having on the five-point scale. The two highest-ranked actors are the EPA's ten regional administrators and the EPA administrator. They have mean influence scores of 4.01 and 3.99, respectively. Interestingly, these are types of presidential appointees. Therefore, consistent with past research (Stewart and Cromartie 1982; Moe 1982; Nathan 1983; Waterman 1989; Wood and Waterman 1991), the evidence here demonstrates that EPA bureaucrats perceive presidential appointees as having considerable influence.

Because the EPA administrator represents the national office and the regional administrators the ten regional offices, we also asked, "If you received contradictory directions from national and regional officials, to whom would you be most likely to respond?" Of the sixty-seven bureaucrats who responded, only 10.4 percent said they would most likely respond to "national/federal EPA officials" while 89.6 percent said they would respond to "EPA regional officials." Thus, while the results in table 4.8 demonstrate that both the EPA administrator and regional administrators are perceived as having considerable influence, we can infer that bureaucrats in the NPDES water program are more likely to defer to the will of the regional administrators and other regional officials rather than to the central EPA headquarters in Washington.

There are other interesting findings in table 4.8 with regard to the perceived influence of Congress and the president. As noted in chapter 3, for many years scholars argued that Congress was incapable of controlling the bureaucracy. Since the 1980s, however, scholarly opinion has ar-

Table 4.8
EPA Personnel Rank the Influence of 14 Political Actors

Principal	Rank	Mean	Standard Deviation
1. EPA regional administrators	1	4.04	0.95
2. EPA administrator	2	3.99	0.97
3. Federal courts	3	3.44	1.10
4. Congress	4	3.36	1.30
5. Environmental groups	5	3.09	1.10
6. Public opinion	6	2.97	1.10
7. President	7	2.84	1.40
8. Permittees	8	2.83	1.03
9. Media	9	2.72	1.10
10. Governors	10	2.71	1.00
11. Business groups	11	2.59	1.10
12. State courts	12	2.50	1.10
13. State legislatures	13	2.31	.090
14. Agricultural groups	14	2.21	1.00

gued that Congress can control it. Our results are consistent with the second viewpoint. In our survey, EPA bureaucrats ranked the Congress fourth overall with a mean influence score of 3.36. On the other hand, the president was ranked seventh with a mean score of just 2.84, barely above the midpoint on the five-point scale. This is more consistent with the old view that the president does not exert influence. Given the high ranking of the president's appointments, and research showing that presidential appointments are one of the president's most effective mechanisms for controlling the bureaucracy, it is clear that presidents do in fact exert influence. Elsewhere Waterman (1999, 155–56) referred to this high ranking of the president's appointees and the president's much lower ranking as the "president-appointee dichotomy." He wrote, "EPA NPDES personnel do not perceive a direct connection between the influence of the president and the influence of the president's own appointees." Consequently, measuring perceptions of presidential influence is a bit more complicated than measuring those of Congress. The president's influence is perceived more indirectly and thus is not as evident to many bureaucrats as is Congress's influence, which is exerted directly through the budgetary, lawmaking, and committee oversight functions.

The results indicate that the federal courts are perceived to be the third most influential actor, exerting even more influence than Congress or the president. Contrarily, the state courts, which have less jurisdiction over federal EPA bureaucrats, are ranked twelfth. While interest groups were long considered to dominate the bureaucratic process, we find variations within types of interest groups: environmental groups rank fifth, business groups eleventh, and agricultural groups fourteenth. In addition, the permittees (the regulated industry), which were central to the capture, iron triangle, and subsystem politics theories, rank only eighth.

Finally, other actors generally not included in either capture, iron triangle or principal-agent models are perceived as having influence at least comparable to that of the president. For example, public opinion ranks just ahead of the president (sixth overall), while the influence of the media ranks ninth, but with a comparable mean of 2.72 in comparison to the president's 2.84. State actors, also are perceived as exerting some influence (governors rank tenth, state courts twelfth, and state legislatures thirteenth).

The results from this chapter indicate that while the governor and state legislature are perceived as having influence at the state level, and while Congress and the president's appointees are seen as having influence at the federal level (both findings consistent with past principal-agent literature), a number of other principals are perceived as exerting influence, as well. While the magnitude of their perceived influence varies, the contact data and perceptions of influence data suggest that, at a minimum, we need to model a variety of political principals at both the state and federal levels when we examine the question of who controls the bureaucracy.

5

A Multiple Principal Model
of Bureaucratic Politics

Principal-agent studies have greatly expanded and enriched our understanding of bureaucratic politics. Yet, like other scholarly models of the bureaucratic process, this theory has its limitations. As argued in chapter 2, many scholars, though not all, have examined principal-agent relationships in a dyadic fashion; one principal and one agent are considered at a time. Yet is this a reasonable way of modeling bureaucratic politics? On this point Moe (1987, 482) writes:

> The simple principal-agent model focuses for convenience on one principal and one agent, highlighting the determinants of control in dyadic relationships. But the extent to which Congress controls a particular agency can hardly be ascertained by riveting attention on the relationship between that agency and on a legislative committee. In fact, the agency finds itself surrounded by multiple principals: various authorizing and appropriations committees in both houses of Congress, the Office of Management and Budget, the president and members of his White House staff, and departmental units in the executive branch. These principals compete for influence over the agency—which, as a result, finds itself under crosspressures, forced to make compromises and trade-offs favoring some principals over others, and, in its own self-interest, attracted to strategies that play its principals off against one another.

Our findings in the last chapter similarly suggest that it is inappropriate to model principal-agent relations in a dyadic factor. Agents for both the EPA and NMED perceive a number of principals as exerting at least some influence over how their office enforces the law. The question, then, is how can we best model these principal interactions? Here we will use a theoretical framework that borrows from Heclo's (1978) idea of "issue networks" and which was further developed by Sabatier and Pelkey (1987), Jenkins-Smith, St. Clair, and Woods (1991), and Sabatier and Jenkins-Smith (1993) as the advocacy coalition model. A major advantage of both of these frameworks is that they specifically allow for the inclusion of multiple principals and even multiple agents, in a model of bureaucratic behavior.

To restate the matter, if various "networks" of political actors exist and interact around different types of "issues," as Heclo (1978) contends, then it also may be useful to think of principals not as separate and distinct political actors, but rather as members of groups of actors who bureaucrats perceive as exerting a similar type of influence (or even as different types of advocacy actors, though perhaps not formal advocacy coalitions, since actors exerting similar types of influence may not advocate the same policy perspective). In this case, groups of principals might be perceived by bureaucrats as having similar interests or as seeking to exert similar types of influence over the bureaucracy. It is to this possibility that we now turn.

The Venues of Influence

The principal-agent model is often presented (or at least empirically tested) as a top-down political model. As such, it tends to address politics hierarchically from the perspective of the political principal. Important here are the motives of the political principal who seeks to control the behavior of their bureaucratic agent. While the agent is perceived to have motives (e.g., a desire to shirk), the agent in empirical principal-agent studies is generally modeled as passive; agents are modeled as either responding to or not responding to principal cues for action. Such assumptions about the motives of agents, however, are based on a dyadic model of political behavior. So long as we are considering only one principal in relationship to one set of agents, and only influence moving in one direction (from principal to agent), such assumptions about the motives of bureaucrats are not entirely unreasonable. Once, however, we move from a dyadic model to a multiple principal model the agents' motives and behavior can become more dynamic and strategic, as well. As Krause (1994, 1999) demonstrates, agents are far from passive participants in the bureaucratic political arena. They play an active role both in terms of setting the policy agenda and in influencing the policy positions of their principals. In addition, as Wood (1988) and Wood and Waterman (1991, 1993, 1994) argue, agents can be strategic actors who can choose to side with principals that most closely represent their policy perspectives. They even can play one principal off against another. We believe these are important points. If, for example, agents do not perceive principals solely as separate and distinct policy actors, but rather as sets of actors who share some type of similar characteristic (such as an interest group member or a hierarchical actor) then bureaucrats may have incentives to respond to different sets of principals in decidedly different ways.

To illustrate this point we use the analogy of a politician and voters. Politicians interact with individual voters, but they rarely treat them as individual voters. Rather they conceptualize them as different groups of voters, each with their own interests and demands. Politicians may make broad based appeals to voters, but they also make specific appeals to different influential constituency groups. Likewise, some constituencies may be ignored altogether. For example, if a politician decides that s/he is unlikely to get a particular group's vote regardless of the effort, or if the cost of winning a group's vote alienates another important constituency group, politicians may decide that active outreach is not warranted.

As with this example, we contend that bureaucratic agents perceive principals as sets of interested constituency groups. Just as a politician identifies different constituencies based on some commonly held voter characteristic (e.g., race, occupation, or income), bureaucrats likewise perceive principals according to specific shared characteristics. Thus, it is possible that bureaucrats perceive judicial actors (e.g., the federal and state courts) as representing one type of constituency, legislative actors (e.g., Congress and the state legislatures) as representing an entirely different type of constituency, interest groups as representing yet another type of constituency, and so on. Or they may perceive state-level principals as representing one type of constituency and federal-level actors as representing another. Likewise, they may consider principals inside government (elected or appointed officials) as one type of constituency and principals outside government (such as interest groups, the public, and the media) as another.

For example, agents at the federal level are expected to respond more substantively to the demands of their hierarchical masters, the president and Congress, since those actors control the budgetary process. They can alter the organizational structure or even abolish an agency such as the EPA. They also enact the legislation that guides the agency's mission. In short, EPA officials have good reasons to pay attention to signals emanating from the White House or Capitol Hill. The same is true of NMED bureaucrats and their relationship with the governor and state legislature who, as we saw in the last chapter, are more likely to use legal directives when they contact agency personnel. Bureaucrats ignore these political actors at their own peril.

On the other hand, EPA bureaucrats have more latitude in responding to policy actors that provide a link with the public or, as we will call them here, linkage mechanisms. These include the media, environmental groups, and the public, all of which can exert outside pressure on the agency. The media can run stories critical of the EPA. Environmental groups can protest what they consider to be adverse agency actions. The public can show its disapproval of EPA activity by writing to legislators. While this influence is important, it is also indirect. The media, environmental groups, and the public generally must seek out alliances with other policy actors (such as the president, Congress, or the courts) if they are to have an impact on EPA activity. These types of principals are more likely to use lower level mechanisms (telephones and faxes) to contact the bureaucracy. Hence, bureaucratic agents may perceive themselves as having greater leeway in dealing with these actors than they do with their hierarchical masters. For this reason, they may not have to respond substantively to demands from linkage mechanism actors. Symbolic responses may, at least temporarily, satisfy (or delay immediate demands) from them. If these actors are later disappointed by these symbolic responses, then they still do not have direct hierarchical control over the EPA. They must still seek out other political principals in order to accomplish their objectives. Thus, it is likely that policy actors who have less hierarchical influence over bureaucratic agents are more likely to receive less substantive and more symbolic responses to their political demands. The empirical evidence from the last chapter supports this point.

On the other hand, legal actors, such as the courts, are expected to receive another sort of attention from their bureaucratic agents. Agents may choose to respond in symbolic ways to linkage mechanisms, or even ignore them, but the courts, with their powerful direct oversight influence, cannot be ignored. Agents have to be sure that the way they write regulations and the manner in which they enforce the law is consistent with past legal doctrine. Bureaucrats also use the courts to bring action against their own agents (in the case of EPA, their permittees) who have violated the law. Thus, the courts can be seen as both a policy actor exerting hierarchical oversight over agency personnel and as a potential enforcement tool. This dual nature for judicial actors necessitates a more technical response to legal principals.

Consequently, identifying the type of influence exerted by a political principal is of critical importance to understanding the relationship between principals and their agents. Agents are much more likely to respond openly and directly to their hierarchical masters, to the president's appointees, and to the courts with their oversight capability, than they are to the various linkage mechanisms, to interest groups (particularly environmental groups), or to state-level politicians. To differentiate this framework from the analogy of an electoral constituency, we call these various bureaucratically perceived associations of principals the venues of influence.

EPA Bureaucrats

We are interested in determining whether there are similarities in agents' perceptions of the influence of political principals. We hypothesized that agents do not perceive influence as being exerted solely by each separate principal in a dyadic fashion, but rather perceive certain types of principals (e.g., interest groups, state-level actors, an agency's hierarchical masters, or political appointees) as exerting similar types of influence. Thus, for example, as we found in the last chapter, while agents from the EPA perceive the federal courts (with a mean influence score of 3.44 on a five-point scale) as exerting more influential than the state courts (with a mean influence score of 2.5), they may still perceive the two principals as exerting a similar type of influence.

For the analysis in this chapter we will further analyze the responses to the question we presented in chapter 4: "How much influence do EPA and NMED bureaucrats perceive various principals as exerting over how their office enforces the law?" (See the results from tables 4.7 and 4.8.) To analyze these data, we will use two statistical techniques: multidimensional scaling and factor analysis. The first of these techniques, multidimensional scaling (MDS) "is designed to analyze distance-like data called dissimilarity data, or data that indicate the degree of dissimilarity (or similarity) of two things" (SPSS 1993, 155). In our case it indicates the degree of dissimilarity between evaluations of the perceived level of influence of the fourteen principals we asked EPA NPDES personnel to rate and the seventeen principals we asked the NMED officials to rate. Once our initial scale is translated into dissimilarity data, MDS analyzes it "in a way that displays the structure of the distance-like data as a geometrical picture" (155). In so doing, the "purpose of MDS is to construct a map of the locations of objects relative to each other from data that specify how different these objects are. This is similar to the problem faced by a surveyor who, once he has surveyed the distances between a set of places, needs to draw a map showing the relative locations of those places" (157). This is calculated by using Euclidian distance to model the dissimilarities between the various principals.

Given our purpose, the mapping of bureaucratic perceptions in multidimensional space is particularly valuable. If agents perceive differences in the influence exerted by various principals, then the MDS mapping should reflect these differences, with the various principals widely dispersed across multidimensional space. On the other hand, if agents perceive similarities, then various principals should be clustered in relative proximity to each other in multidimensional space.

We turn our attention first to an analysis of the 1994 survey of bureaucratic agents from the EPA NPDES program. A stress statistic of 0.05 (or less) indicates that it is appropriate to model the perceptions of our fourteen principals in five-dimensional space. We present the data for each dimension in table 5.1. For ease of visual presentation, in figure 5.1 we employ a map or geometric picture of the proximity placements of each principal in two-dimensional space. We then refer to table 5.1 to identify any differences that occur as we move across additional dimensions of space.

The map in two-dimensional space was created by placing the calculated dissimilarities for dimension 1 on the x-axis and the dissimilarities for dimension 2 on the y-axis. It should be interpreted like a map; that is, EPA bureaucrats perceive similarities in the influence exerted by those

Table 5.1
Results of the Multidimensional Scaling: EPA Survey

	Dimension				
	1	2	3	4	5
President	−0.72	−0.42	−0.29	0.01	0.20
Congress	−0.58	−0.33	−0.31	0.06	0.28
EPA administrator	−0.39	−0.18	0.57	0.10	−0.31
Regional administrators	−0.27	0.13	0.75	0.04	0.14
Federal courts	−0.28	0.66	-0.01	0.00	−0.05
State courts	−0.06	0.55	-0.19	0.09	−0.03
State legislatures	−0.01	0.38	-0.34	0.13	−0.13
Governors	−0.04	−0.10	−0.08	0.11	−0.26
Agriculture groups	0.08	−0.11	−0.04	−0.65	−0.17
Business groups	0.30	−0.12	−0.09	−0.58	−0.12
Environmental groups	0.41	−0.11	0.05	0.26	-0.29
Media	0.46	−0.18	−0.23	0.33	−0.04
Public opinion	0.59	−0.39	0.18	0.21	0.12
Permittees	0.50	0.22	0.13	−0.10	0.66

principals who are located in close proximity to each other in figure 5.1. The further apart two principals are, the more dissimilar their influence is considered to be. Our fourteen principals map into the four quadrants of multidimensional space. For simplicity's sake we identify them as quadrants A, B, C, and D.

We are interested in determining how bureaucrats perceive their principals relative to each other. A perusal of figure 5.1 is the first evidence that bureaucrats do indeed perceive multiple principals in a structured manner. In quadrant D, for example, the president and Congress, the two so-called hierarchical masters of the bureaucracy, map together in relative proximity to each other. The principal-agent literature has tended to examine the interrelationship of these two political principals. Figure 5.1 provides evidence that bureaucrats also perceive a similar type of interrelationship.

The two types of EPA appointees also map close to each other. Interestingly, however, the EPA administrator and the regional administrator map closer to Congress than they do to the president. This suggests, that for whatever reason, EPA NPDES enforcement personnel do not draw a direct connection between the president's influence and that of his appointees (see also Waterman 1999). In addition, the regional administrators, who represent more parochial interests than does the EPA adminis-

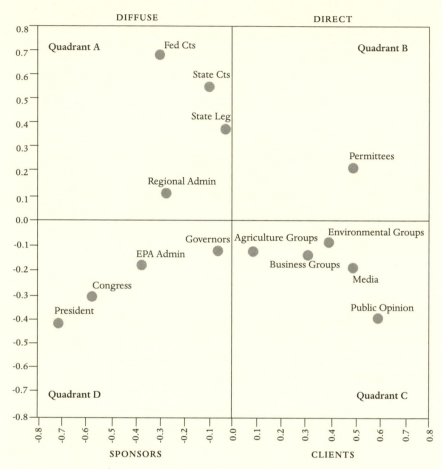

Figure 5.1: Map of the Perceptions of the Influence of 14 Principals by EPA NPDES Enforcement Personnel

trator, map closer to the three state-level actors than to any of the three federal actors. In fact, the regional administrators map as close to the governors and state legislatures as they do the EPA administrator, while the EPA administrator maps closer to two federal actors responsible for her appointment—Congress and the president. This proximity mapping identifies an important difference in the way EPA NPDES personnel perceive these two types of appointees. Clearly, agency personnel perceive the EPA administrator as more of a federal actor while the regional administrator is seen as more of a state actor. This finding is consistent with

Hunter and Waterman's (1996) conclusion, as well as our own unstructured interviews, in which top officials from the EPA said that regional administrators tend to be more concerned with the interests of the various states in their regions than with overall federal policy.

In quadrant A, the federal and state courts also map closely together; this is clear evidence that bureaucrats perceive both actors as exerting a similar type of influence. Likewise, the state legislatures map near to the state courts. It is also interesting to note that while the governors are somewhat distant from the state legislatures and state courts in multidimensional space, they do map along the same vertical line as the state legislatures. Thus, we have evidence that EPA NPDES personnel do perceive a similarity in the type of influence exerted by various state-level actors, though governors are seen as somewhat different from the state courts and legislatures.

The governors also map close to three interest groups we asked our respondents to evaluate. Agriculture, business, and environmental groups map horizontally across quadrant C, with the material interest groups (business and agriculture groups) mapping closest to the governors, while the purposive groups (environmental) map closest to the media and public opinion.[1] Why would governors map in relative proximity to interest groups? According to open-ended interviews we conducted with EPA NPDES personnel, governors are perceived by federal environmental personnel as lobbyists who, lacking direct hierarchical control over EPA personnel, seek to influence their behavior much as do other interest groups. Therefore, their influence is perceived as of a similar type as that of the interest groups.

As noted, the environmental groups also map vertically in quadrant C with the media and public opinion, or what are commonly considered to be linkage mechanisms. This is an interesting finding since we would expect that environmental groups would be more willing to use the media, and to reach out to public opinion, than either business or agriculture groups. It is thus interesting to reiterate that the environmental groups are closest in proximity to the media and the public, while the two material interest groups map more distantly from them.

Finally, the NPDES permittees, or regulated industry, which also can be considered as an agent of EPA personnel, are located alone in quadrant B. Counter to the assumptions of the capture or iron triangle theories, they do not map close to the U.S. Congress. In fact, of all the fourteen principals we asked the EPA personnel to evaluate, the permittees seem to be the most dissimilar from the others, suggesting that they can perform the functions of both a principal and an agent. They do map closer to the interest groups than to any other type of principal, but they do not map with them. In short, the influence of the NPDES permittees, or the regulated industry that EPA personnel interact with on a daily basis, is seen as more separate and distinct than the influence of any of the other principals.

As we have noted, figure 5.1 presents the results of the MDS analysis in simple two-dimensional space. To determine how valid it is to represent the fourteen principals in this simplified manner we also need to examine table 5.1 for the coefficients for each of the other three dimensions; the coefficients for the president and Congress on the third dimension are -0.29 and -0.31 respectively, on the fourth dimension 0.01 and 0.06 respectively, and on the fifth dimension 0.20 and 0.28 respectively. As these figures demonstrate, the president and Congress continue to map closely together throughout multidimensional space. Likewise, an examination of the coefficients in table 5.1 indicate that the EPA and regional administrators map closely together on dimensions three and four, However, they map in different quadrants on the fifth dimension, which may represent a recognition of the more parochial interests of the regional administrators versus the national focus of the EPA administrator. With regard to other principals, the federal and state courts map in close proximity to each other on the other three dimensions, as do the state courts and state legislatures. Meanwhile, the governors and material interest groups continue to map together on the other three dimensions. As we would expect, differences do emerge between the coefficients for the material and purposive interest groups on dimension four, with environmental groups continuing to map close to the media along subsequent dimensions. Finally, and somewhat unexpectedly, differences emerge between the media and public opinion on the third and fifth dimensions. Thus, while some differences do become apparent as we move through multidimensional space, in general it is apparent that figure 5.1 reliably represents our bureaucrats' perceived relationships of the influence of their various principals.

The results from table 5.1 and figure 5.1 provide a first empirical clue as to how agents perceive their political principals in proximity to each other. We had hypothesized that agents would perceive their principals, not solely as separate and distinct political actors, but rather as groups of actors sharing some type of common political characteristic. We have found that EPA NPDES enforcement personnel do indeed perceive similarities in the influence exerted by different principals. For example, the close proximity in which the president and Congress map together is evidence that bureaucratic agents perceive a similarity in the influence exerted by these two principals. Similarly, the relative propinquity in which the federal and state courts map suggests that agents perceive similarities in their influences. Likewise, the state courts, state legislatures, and the governors line up vertically in multidimensional space, which is evidence of a similarity in bureaucratic perceptions of the influence for these three principals. We also find that agents perceive material interest groups in similar ways and see a connection between the influence of environmental groups and the media, and, to a lesser extent, public opinion. Finally, we find that agents perceive similarities in the influence of the EPA administrator and the regional administrators.

The proximity measures also tell us something about the differences or distinctiveness of perceptions of principal influence. For example, the fact that the courts map in an entirely different quadrant from interest groups and linkage mechanisms is evidence that agents do not perceive the courts as exerting the same type of influence as either of those two principals, or for that matter as the president and Congress.

Furthermore, if we compare the left and right sides of figure 5.1, we find that all of the principals located on the left side (in quadrants A and D) are governmental actors, either elected or appointed. In other words, they are all, to some degree, sponsors of the EPA NPDES program. In contrast, all of the principals on the right side of figure 5.1 are nongovernmental actors and thus, to one degree or another, represent various clients (broadly defined) of the EPA NPDES program. Permittees and interest groups are or can be directly regulated by EPA NPDES personnel. The public, through its intermediary the media or directly through public opinion, is also a client of the EPA in that the agency ultimately is supposed to serve the public interest. EPA NPDES personnel, then, answer to each of the principals on the left side of figure 5.1, while they serve all of the principals on the right side of the figure. In addition, those principals or sponsors who are more likely to serve as clients as well as sponsors, especially the governors, map closest to the axis separating the right and left sides of the figure. To us, the division of principals into sponsors and clients is the most interesting means by which agents' perceptions of their principals can be grouped.

The picture is a bit less clear when we compare the top half (quadrants A and B) to the bottom half (quadrants C and D) of figure 5.1. EPA NPDES personnel have more direct interactions with the principals in quadrants A and B, particularly their regional administrators and the permittees they regulate. The EPA NPDES personnel have to deal with the courts, as decisions are rendered in individual cases and regulations are challenged. Since they serve in regional offices, and are assigned responsibilities to supervise or interact with specific states, they also may have considerable interactions with the state officials, such as the state legislatures, which can set more stringent standards than exist at the national level.

Less direct or more diffuse contacts are expected with the principals in the lower half of figure 5.1 (quadrants C and D). Although the president and Congress are the direct hierarchical masters of the EPA, NPDES personnel do not interact daily with either of these principals. Likewise, NPDES personnel have far less regular contact with the EPA administrator than they do with their regional administrators. Thus, in addition to the client/sponsor dichotomy in figure 5.1, there may be a direct/diffuse dichotomy that is related to the frequency of interaction between EPA NPDES personnel interact and various principals.

In table 5.2 we examine the perceptions of EPA NPDES personnel in yet another manner; we use factor analysis to analyze the EPA survey

Table 5.2
Rotated Factor Scores for the EPA Survey

Factor	Factor Score	Factor	Factor Score
1: Hierarchical masters		*4: Appointees*	
President	.97	Regional administrators	.94
Congress	.96	EPA administrators	.81
2: Legal actors		*5: Material interest groups*	
Federal courts	.99	Business groups	.94
State courts	.87	Agricultural groups	.93
State legislatures	.73	*6: Regulated industry*	
3: Linkage mechanisms		Permittees	.87
Media	.90		
Public opinion	.87		
Environmental groups	.83		

data. The results are strikingly similar to what we found in figure 5.1 and table 5.1. The president and Congress load together on one dimension: the traditional principal-agent factor. The federal courts, state courts, and state legislatures load on a second factor, with the EPA and regional administrators loading together on yet another factor. Again, each of these principals is a sponsor of the EPA NPDES program. With regard to the NPDES program's clients, the media, public opinion, and environmental groups load on one factor, the material interest groups on a second factor, and as was the case in Figure 5.1, permittees load alone on their own separate factor. So once again we find the same distinction between sponsors and clients. In short, the evidence from tables 5.1 and 5.2 and figure 5.1 is consistent with regard to how EPA NPDES enforcement personnel perceive the various principals we asked them to rate.

NMED Bureaucrats

In table 5.3 we present the results of the multidimensional-scaling model for seventeen principals with whom the officials of the New Mexico Environment Department interact. We also present the model in two-dimensional space in figure 5.2 (although the results actually map into four-dimensional space—see table 5.3). A comparison of figures 5.1 and 5.2 indicates that there are interesting similarities between the perceptions of federal and state bureaucrats. As with their federal counterparts, state-level bureaucrats perceive the two EPA appointees (the EPA administrator and the administrator for region six, who oversees the New Mexico Environment Department) as mapping closely together in multidimensional space. Likewise, for NMED bureaucrats, the president and Congress map together, as do the material interest groups, the state and federal courts, and the media and public opinion. All of these findings are consistent with the perceptions of federal bureaucrats.

These similarities are even more striking if we rotate the x-axis for figure 5.1 clockwise by two quadrants such that Quadrant D of Figure 5.1 is in the same multidimensional space as quadrant B of figure 5.2. When we do so, the Congress, the president, and the EPA administrator are located in the same quadrants in the two figures. Likewise, once we have rotated the x-axis two quadrants clockwise, quadrants A of figure 5.1 and C of figure 5.2 match. The federal and state courts are located in

Table 5.3
Results of the Multidimensional Scaling: NMED Survey

	Dimension			
	1	2	3	4
President	0.32	0.03	0.29	−0.35
Congress	0.46	0.10	0.23	−0.37
EPA administrator	0.12	0.06	−0.31	0.01
Regional administrator	0.22	0.00	−0.46	−0.19
Federal courts	0.53	−0.02	−0.22	0.19
State courts	0.44	−0.14	−0.30	0.32
State legislature	0.13	−0.48	0.14	0.10
Legislative Finance Committee	−0.32	−0.43	0.14	−0.11
Department of Finance and Administration	−0.31	−0.38	0.08	−0.17
Governor	−0.01	−0.05	0.11	−0.05
Agriculture groups	−0.06	0.12	0.07	0.45
Business groups	−0.18	0.08	0.14	0.52
Environmental groups	0.31	0.30	0.27	−0.04
Media	−0.25	0.38	0.31	0.08
Public opinion	−0.19	0.43	0.25	−0.06
County commissioners	−0.54	0.19	−0.25	−0.04
Mayors	−0.42	0.24	−0.50	−0.29

both of these quadrants. Likewise, the regional administrators are located in quadrant A of figure 5.1 and are located on the axis between quadrant B and quadrant C of figure 5.2. Also, when we rotate the axis to compare quadrant C of figure 5.1 with quadrant A of figure 5.2, we see that agricultural and business interest groups, the media, and the public all are in the same quadrants.

While there are remarkable similarities between the perceptions of federal and state personnel, some differences do emerge between the two sets of bureaucratic agents. Although environmental groups map close to the media and to public opinion for EPA NPDES personnel, this is not the case for NMED bureaucrats. Similarly, NMED employees do not place, the state legislature close to the state courts.

In figure 5.2 we also examine some policy actors we did not consider in figure 5.1. We examine two local-level political principals, mayors and county commissioners, who map closely together in quadrant A of Figure 5.2. Likewise, three state-level actors, the New Mexico state legislature, the Legislative Finance Committee (LFC), and the Department of Finance and Administration (DFA) map closely together in quadrant D.

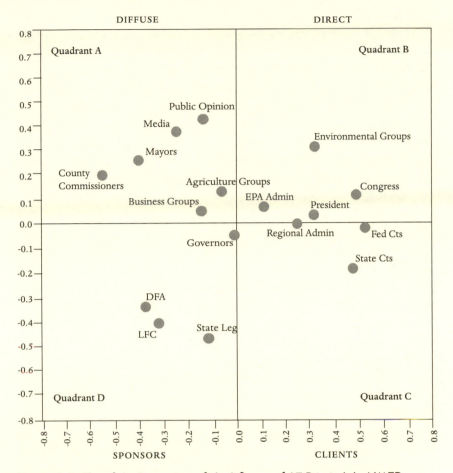

Figure 5.2: Map of the Perceptions of the Influence of 17 Principals by NMED Bureaucrats

While the governor does not map directly with these three state-level actors, he does map in the same quadrant as them.

A perusal of table 5.3 indicates that with the exception of the EPA and regional administrator on dimension four, and, to a lesser extent, the media and public opinion on the same dimension, perceptions of these various actors continue to map in close proximity across subsequent dimensions. Thus we are confident that the picture that emerges in figure 5.2 is a reliable indicator of the actual perceptions of NMED personnel.

As was the case with federal EPA bureaucrats, we can divide the quadrants in figure 5.2 into clients and sponsors for NMED personnel. This time the client/sponsor dichotomy is found in the top and bottom halves of the figure. All of the actors in quadrants C and D are sponsors or hierarchical principals of NMED personnel. These include all of the state-level actors plus the federal courts. The principals in quadrants A and B do not exert direct hierarchical influence over NMED personnel. For example, interest groups and linkage mechanisms may exert pressure, but they do not do so hierarchically. Unless new legislation is enacted, or funding formulas for grants to the states are altered, the president and the Congress, while they are hierarchical principals of EPA bureaucrats, do not have the same level of direct control over state-level bureaucrats; in contrast, the federal courts, through its rulings, can exert direct hierarchical control over state agencies. Likewise, the EPA administrator does not have direct hierarchical control. The regional administrator for region six, who is not hierarchically superior to NMED personnel, is closer in proximity to NMED bureaucrats (located in the EPA office in Denver) and hence has more direct influence over the NMED program. Rather interestingly, then, the regional administrator is located directly on the x-axis between the top and bottom of figure 5.2. Finally, while mayors and county commissioners are elected officials, they do not have direct hierarchical influence over NMED personnel. They act, rather, as clients who seek favors, not as sponsors with hierarchical political control.

In figure 5.2 we also see clear evidence of the direct/diffuse dichotomy. Looking from left to right across figure 5.2, in quadrants A and D it is apparent that all of the principals are local actors and thus can directly interact with NMED personnel. Four of the five state-level principals fall on the left side of figure 5.2, with only the state courts on the right side of the figure. Likewise, the two locally elected officials (mayors and county commissioners) are on the left side of figure 5.2. In figure 5.1 the media, interest groups, and the public were considered to be diffuse actors who did not interact directly with the federal-level personnel. At the state level, however, such interactions are much more intimate. That is, state personnel are more likely to interact directly with these actors than are federal personnel. For example, when NMED personnel deal with business or agriculture groups, they deal predominantly with interest groups from New Mexico. Likewise, when they consider the media and public opinion, they are mostly concerned with media outlets in

New Mexico and the opinions of New Mexico citizens. We note, then, that each of these principals is represented on the left side of figure 5.2.

On the right side of Figure 5.2 most of the principals are national actors (the president, the Congress, and the federal courts), and the two EPA administrators. While environmental groups have local chapters, they tend to be more national in focus than either the business or agriculture groups with which NMED personnel regularly interact. Hence, it is not too unreasonable to classify them as national and thus more diffuse political actors. The only major exception to this direct/diffuse distinction, then, is the state courts. That they should be seen in relative proximity with other national actors is not clear to us; perhaps this reflects their judicial function, which is not easily subject to the lobbying efforts of traditional local politics. Still, the evidence in figure 5.2 is strong with regard to the direct/diffuse dichotomy. Additionally, in both figures there is clear evidence of a client/sponsor dichotomy.

In short, the relative placement of the actors in figures 5.1 and 5.2 is convincing evidence that bureaucrats at both the federal and state level do not perceive the principals with which they interact solely as separate and distinct entities. Rather, they perceive similarities between various principals based on their function (material interest groups, linkage mechanisms, courts, appointees, local officials, state officials, and traditional hierarchical masters), whether they are sponsors or clients of the agency, and whether the principals have direct or diffuse contact with agents.

In table 5.4 we present the results of the factor analysis of the NMED survey. As was the case in quadrant D of figure 5.2, with the exception of the state courts, the other four state-level principals load together. The president and Congress again load together, but since they are no longer perceived as direct, hierarchical actors, they load on the same factor with other sponsors that exert diffuse influence (i.e., environmental groups, the media, and the public). The media and the public also load on the same factor with two other diffuse principals (i.e., the local-level actors; the mayors and county commissioners). The only puzzling result from table 5.4 is that the federal and state courts load on the same factor with the two presidential appointees. Still, for the most part, as was the case with the results of table 5.2, the results from the factor analysis are consistent with our multi-dimensional scaling results.

The evidence from both the federal and state level surveys, then, is consistent with our hypothesis. Bureaucratic agents do not perceive prin-

Table 5.4
Rotated Factor Scores for the NMED Survey

Factor	Factor Score	Factor	Factor Score
1: Linkage mechanisms and		*3: State actors*	
EPA hierarchical masters		State legislature	.76
Congress	.74	Governor	.73
President	.67	Legislative Finance	
Environmental groups	.73	Committee	.84
Media	.60	Department of Finance	
Public opinion	.58	and Administration	.82
2: Legal and appointees'		*4: Local influences*	
influences		Media	.55
Federal courts	.82	Public opinion	.52
State courts	.75	Mayors	.86
EPA administrator	.69	County commissioners	.85
Regional administrator	.67		

cipals solely as separate and distinct actors, as has been the common modeling practice in the principal-agent literature. Rather, agents perceive various principals as exerting similar characteristics. At both levels, bureaucratic agents draw a clear distinction between sponsors and clients. To a somewhat lesser extent, they also see distinctions between whether actors exert direct or diffuse influence over how their office enforces the law. Finally, both federal and state bureaucrats perceive similarities in the influence exerted by Congress and the president, the EPA and regional administrators, material interest groups, the courts, and linkage mechanisms.

Our results suggest that we need to model a variety of principals and not just the president, Congress, and the courts. Likewise, our analysis shows that we should conceptualize principals by the type of influence they exert. This is an important finding since past empirical research assumes that agents are expected to respond in the same way to a variety of different principals. As a result, if no relationship is found between a principal and the number of enforcement actions conducted by agency personnel, it is assumed that agents did not respond to that principal and therefore that the principal had no influence. What we argue here is that agents have incentives to respond in different ways to different types of principals. This means that a reliance on any one kind of response measure is not entirely appropriate. While the number of enforcement actions may not change when interest groups put pressure on an agency, bureaucrats may respond to these groups in other important ways.

In conclusion, once we move to a multiple principal model of bureaucratic politics we need to consider not only different types of political principals, but also the different ways bureaucrats are likely to respond to them. The analysis in chapter 4 provided some empirical evidence on this point, suggesting that agents are contacted in different ways by different kinds of principals and that some principals use higher-level mechanisms (e.g., legal directives) to contact agents. We can expect that agents are aware of the different means by which they are contacted, the different levels of hierarchical authority that different principals possess, whether the principal is a client or a sponsor, and politically how close the agent is to the principal (e.g., whether they are likely to initiate diffuse or direct contact). All of these factors contribute to the development of differential perceptions of the type of principal influence over the bureaucracy and need to be incorporated into a more dynamic principal-agent interaction. Static dyadic models simply are not realistic.

6

Bureaucrats' Knowledge of Their Budgets

Thus far we have concentrated on an analysis of the principal-agent model and the implications of adding multiple principals to it. As we noted in chapter 3, however, another major bureaucratic theory is William Niskanen's idea that bureaucrats are budget-maximizers. Niskanen (1971) argues that bureaucrats strive to maximize budgets rather than achieve policy goals or pursue other incentives. For this reason, we are interested in how much knowledge bureaucrats have about their own agency's budget. Since Niskanen's thesis focuses on the idea that agency personnel are interested in developing "slack resources"—an inefficient resource base above what they actually need to perform their bureaucratic tasks—one would expect that bureaucrats would know what they need and then exceed that amount in order to develop slack resources.

How Much Do Bureaucrats Know about the Budget?

The heart of Niskanen's microeconomics-based approach to explaining what motivates the behavior of bureaucrats is the assertion that, since budgets confer benefits on bureaucrats, bureaucrats must act to maximize their agency's budget in order to maximize their personal utility. The budget-maximizer theory does not require that specific actions be taken by individuals informed by conscious knowledge of the budgetary ramifications of all potential bureaucratic actions. Yet if the budget-maximization model is to be an empirically convincing one, it is reasonable to expect members to have a keen awareness of fluctuations in the bureau's budget. Even more convincing evidence for the budget-maximization thesis would result from evidence that bureaucrats perceive themselves as benefiting from the budgetary gains of the bureau as a whole. Such an identification between the individual bureau member's personal utility and the budget increases of the bureau as a whole is also central to the framework.

The logical starting point for discovering how much knowledge bureaucrats possess about their agency's budget might be to ask the question directly, for example: What is your agency's budget for the current fiscal year? Searching for an ability to cite specific figures, something that even a budget specialist would probably have trouble doing without reference, does not seem, however, to be a valid approach to the overall question. It calls for a great deal of specific knowledge, which we believe most employees will not have. A better test of bureaucrats' budget knowledge is bureaucratic perceptions of variations in their agency's budget over a short period of time. One might not know one's overall budget, but it is likely that one would know whether funding has been increasing or decreasing over the short term. If one sees layoffs and cutbacks, then one can assume that the agency's budget is being trimmed. If one hears members of Congress calling for budgetary constraint, then one can assume that the agency's budget is being reduced. On the other hand, if one sees new personnel arriving and expanded regulatory functions, then one can assume that the budget is increasing. Thus, much less knowledge is required for a bureaucrat to make a determination that their agency budget has increased, decreased, or stayed the same over a short period of time than would be required to identify the actual dimensions of the agency budget. Since budgets vary over time, and responses to budget-related cues must be perpetual, it is reasonable to expect that the budget-maximizing bureau member would have a well-informed perception of the variations in the bureau's resource situation over a period of time. We contend that if bureau members are budget-maximizers, they have an incentive to be attentive to budget matters.

To provide a measure of the bureaucrats' knowledge of general variations in their agency's budget, EPA and NMED members were asked two questions: "Please indicate whether you think the EPA budget has increased, decreased, or stayed about the same in the last five years (controlling for inflation)." This was followed by, "By what percent do you think the budget has increased or decreased in the last five years?" The survey instructions specifically asked respondents to give their opinions and estimates without consulting any sources or other individuals.

In examining budgetary knowledge we also considered whether each respondent had supervisory or managerial duties versus responsibilities of a purely technical nature. We did so because the revised version of the Niskanen theory predicts that those employees who have actual control or oversight of budget resources, that is, supervisory or managerial personnel, will be likely to possess a higher degree of knowledge regarding their budgets than those with strictly technical positions. While the EPA sample represents highly technical personnel, enough respondents with supervisory and fiscal duties were included to examine this possibility. The NMED sample is much broader and includes administrative and financial personnel. NMED respondents were coded by technical versus managerial job types in order to examine differences between the groups. We also expected that those members who perceived a direct relationship between the budget recommendations of the agency's sponsors and the behavior of the agency would be more likely to be knowledgeable about the budget in general.

Finally, analysis was undertaken for the purpose of controlling for standard demographic characteristics. The demographic variables included in both surveys were the respondent's age, years of service at the agency, gender, household income level, educational level, and educational field. NMED employees also were asked their racial/ethnic identification. Also, EPA and NMED employees were asked how long they had worked for their agencies. This was done to specifically test if budgetary knowledge is related to length of service with an agency. The hypothesis is that the longer one has worked for an agency (EPA or NMED) the greater his or her knowledge of the budget will be.

Since the EPA is divided nationally into ten regions, eight of which responded to the survey, we also asked EPA personnel in which region they worked. Previous research, such as that of Scholz, Twombly, and Headrick (1991) and Hunter and Waterman (1996), suggests that variations in bureaucratic behavior might be tied to geographical and regional factors related to federal bureaucracies.

Analysis and Results: The Environmental Protection Agency

The responses from EPA officials were received from March through August of 1994. This period spans the middle to the near end of fiscal year 1994 ending on September 30, 1994. In the five years preceding the questionnaire responses, from fiscal 1990 through fiscal 1994 (the last three years of the presidency of George H. W. Bush and the first two years of Bill Clinton's first term), the EPA's budget allocation increased from $5.108 billion to $5.855 billion, an increase of 14.6 percent unadjusted for inflation (U.S. Department of Labor, Bureau of Labor Statistics). The compounded rate of inflation during that same period, as measured by the consumer price index average for all measured goods and services, was 19.3 percent; the budget therefore actually declined by 4.7 percent in real dollars during the period in question.

Relatively few bureau members were aware of their agency's actual budget variation; less than one-third (22) of those who responded thought, correctly, that the agency's budget had in fact decreased; a type of knowledge that, as we have noted, would require relatively little attentiveness to budgetary matters. Slightly more (26 members) erroneously thought that the budget for the agency had increased in the past five years, while a few (16) respondents thought the budget had remained "about the same."

Table 6.1 presents the respondents' perceptions of budget increases or decreases with respondents' estimated percentage of change in one direction or the other. Negative values indicate decreases in the budget, while positive values indicate increases, and zero indicates that the budget remained unchanged. Reference to this table shows that one respondent specified an increase of only 2 percent. The table also shows that fourteen of the sixteen respondents who said the budget had "stayed pretty much the same" clarified their answers by specifying a 0 percent change. Only two respondents were virtually correct in their answer that the budget had decreased by 5 percent.

Two facts are striking about the data presented in the table. One is how little knowledge there was among respondents as to whether the agency's budget in the preceding five years had in fact declined at all. More bureau members, 39 percent of the total, were of the impression that the EPA's budget had increased, controlling for inflation, than thought it had decreased in the same time. Less than one-third correctly thought

Table 6.1
Estimated Levels of the EPA's Budgetary Increase or Decrease 1990–1994 (N = 59)

Estimated Level (%) + or –	Frequency	Valid Percent
−40	1	1.7
−25	1	1.7
−20	4	6.8
−15	6	10.2
−12.5	1	1.7
−10	5	8.5
−5	**2**	**3.4**
0 (stayed the same)	16	27.1
2	1	1.7
5	4	6.8
10	4	6.8
15	2	3.4
20	7	11.9
25	2	3.4
30	1	1.7
40	1	1.7
50	1	1.7
Total	59	100.0

Note: Bold = correct estimation.

that the budget had gotten smaller. The second surprising fact is how wide the variation was among respondents in the amount of budgetary change in either direction. Decreases of as much as 40 percent and increases of up to 50 percent were reported. It is difficult to imagine that such drastic changes in either direction would not be readily apparent to any observer, and given the modest actual figure, such dramatic variation in estimates certainly does not indicate a high level of knowledge overall. In the final analysis, however, three-fifths of the personnel, 59 percent, were within a range of plus or minus ten points on either side of the accurate estimate of plus or minus 5 percent. This certainly reflects a greater degree of budget awareness, especially from a sample of technical personnel. Still, extrapolating from the Niskanen thesis, one would expect greater knowledge of the budget from a larger percentage of agency personnel; the fact that 41 percent of agency personnel still were not within 10 percent, in either direction, of the actual budget change figure cannot be considered as strong evidence for the Niskanen thesis.[1]

Independent Variables and Budget Knowledge

To identify people with supervisory or fiscal duties, two questions were asked. The first question asked was, "Does your job include supervising other enforcement or compliance personnel?" The second question was, "Does your job include grant tracking or administration?"

Although grants are, by definition, not part of the bureau's budget, those whose jobs involve administering them are primarily concerned with financial matters, and are thus "managers" according to Niskanen's criteria in that they control their own "budgets." These first two variables, occupation of supervisory or grant-tracking roles, were examined although a relatively small number of respondents held such positions (eleven had grant-tracking responsibilities, twelve were supervisors of other personnel). We also examined those bureau members who directly expressed the opinion that the bureau's behavior *does* affect the agency's budget recommendations. We posited that since they saw a direct connection between the bureau's behavior and its budgetary allocations, they would have greater knowledge of the budget. A series of questions included on the survey referred specifically to whether "the way in which the EPA/NMED enforces the law now affects how much money (the sponsor) will recommend for the EPA in the future."

The sponsors were the congressional appropriations committees, the president, and the Office of Management and Budget. The responses regarding the last two sponsors were so closely correlated that they were combined into one "executive" variable for analysis. Nevertheless, the executive variable never demonstrated statistical significance in any iteration of the model.

Employees' sense of being tied to the agency might be relevant to their knowledge of funding issues. With this in mind, we also examined whether or not a respondent was willing to take a job in another federal agency or in the regulated sector. Neither of these variables demonstrated a statistically significant relationship to budget accuracy through difference of means analyses.

Lastly, given the Niskanen model's assumption that bureau employees receive direct benefits from budget increases, it follows that those who would expect to benefit in some immediate sense from a budget increase would have a greater incentive to be attentive to the budget than those who would not. Difference of means tests did not demonstrate that personnel in supervisory roles would be more accurate than others in their estimates of budget variation. Although supervisors were, on average, more accurate than non-supervisors in their estimates of budget variation, the difference of means of the accuracy between estimates made by the two groups was not significant. There was a statistically significant difference of means in accuracy between respondents who were responsible for tracking grants and those who were not, however. Interestingly, and unexpectedly, those who tracked grants were *less* accurate in their estimations of budgetary variation than those who did not (means = 20 and 12.6 respectively). While the expectation that grant trackers would be significantly more accurate than others was not particularly strong, given that those who track grant money are dealing with funding independent of the agency's budget, certainly a significant relationship in the opposite direction was not foreseen. Why the administrators of grants would be significantly less accurate in their agency budget assessments is not readily apparent. Perhaps those who track grants erroneously make a connection between grant funding levels, of which they must be aware, and agency budgets.

There was multicollinearity between the responses regarding the effect of bureau behavior on the budget recommendations of the Clinton administration and the OMB. As a result, these variables were combined. There were interesting differences between response sets. Those who agreed with the statement, "The way the agency enforces the law now affects how much money the executive branch sponsors will recommend for the EPA budget in the future," were much more accurate in their budget assessments than those who strongly disagreed. The difference of means was not statistically significant overall, (possibly due to a small number of responses in the strongly disagree category), still this suggests that bureaucrats who perceive that the manner in which their offices carry out their mandates does affect the agency's budget recommendations from direct sponsors are more attuned to fluctuations in the budget than those who do not perceive such an influence. When responses to the same statement are related to congressional appropriations committees there is a significant difference, reflecting the same pattern; those who strongly agreed that the agency's behavior influences committee recommendations were also much more accurate in their budget assessments than those who strongly disagreed with the statement.

The results from difference of means tests provided no evidence of a relationship between any of the demographic factors and knowledge of the agency budget. Also, no evidence was found to support the hypothesis that the longer one was employed at the EPA the greater one's knowledge of the budget would be. Finally, we examined the possibility that differences existed between the eight responding EPA regions. While there was some variation in the distribution of responses among regions, difference of means tests both showed that there were no statistically significant relationships between members' regional assignments and their perceptions of the agency's budget.

To ameliorate a possible small "N" problem, an alternative examination was conducted, which collapsed the eight regions covered in our survey into four geographically contiguous combined regions. Yet again, no significant differences were revealed in the accuracy of budget knowledge.

Do Bureaucrats Benefit from Their Budgets?

It already has been shown that the budgetary knowledge of EPA personnel is limited. The next question is, even if their knowledge of the budget is limited, do EPA personnel perceive themselves as benefiting from agency budget increases? To get at this question we asked EPA personnel, "If the EPA's budget were to be increased by 10 percent, do you think your regional office would benefit in any way?" While the Niskanen thesis can survive the charge that bureaucrats are not knowledgeable about the budget (they may simply want more), the question of personal benefit is central to the Niskanen thesis. Yet, if bureaucrats perceive no benefit for budget increases, then a major assumption of the theory has been undercut.

While 41 respondents, or 69 percent, said that it would benefit their office, 18 respondents, or 31 percent, said that it would not. Thus, a considerable percentage of EPA personnel do not perceive a connection between budgets and a perceived benefit. This is not consistent with the basic Niskanen assumption, which posits that all bureaucrats are budget-maximizers, though it may still be consistent with the revised Niskanen thesis, which places a greater emphasis on supervisory personnel only. In addition, we found that those who did expect personal benefit from such an agency gain were no more knowledgeable regarding budget variation than those who did not. Interestingly, there also was no relationship between EPA bureaucrats' own expected utility from a 10 percent budget increase and the accuracy of their budget perceptions.

Because the budget-maximizer thesis relies on the mutual identification by bureaucrats of their personal benefit and the benefit of their agencies, it follows that bureaucrats should not be eager to leave their agencies. Too wide a "revolving door" between public and private sectors, or between public agencies, erodes the assumption of member-bureau mutual interest. The Niskanen model requires perceptions of a relatively high level of inseparability between the individual and the organization by the individual bureaucrat. Responses to two yes/no survey questions were included in the test of the Niskanen thesis here. One asked whether the respondent would be willing to take a higher paying job in another federal agency, the other if the respondent would be willing to take a higher paying job in the regulated industry. The expectation is that those employees less likely to leave the agency would be more likely to identify with the agency, and therefore would be more knowledgeable regarding its budget.

It is possible that those who did not expect to receive a benefit from increased agency spending were also those who were more likely to be willing to take a job with another federal agency or the regulated industry. We therefore cross-tabulated whether one expected a benefit, first with whether one would be willing to take a job in another federal agency and then with a willingness to be employed by the regulated industry. In both cases, the chi-square values indicate no statistically significant relationship, meaning that these individuals were no more likely than those who planned to stay with the agency to perceive a benefit from budgetary increases. Neither was it related to the number of years one had worked for the EPA.

Our findings, then, show that there is considerable disagreement among EPA NPDES personnel regarding whether their budget has increased, decreased, or stayed the same. Likewise, there are widely different estimates of presumed increases or decreases in the budget over time. Nearly a third of EPA bureaucrats did not expect to receive a benefit if their office's budget increased by 10 percent. In short, these findings suggest that EPA bureaucrats have relatively low levels of knowledge about their own budget and that while some bureaucrats may be motivated by their budgets, it likely is not the only factor that motivates them.

Budget Knowledge: New Mexico Environment Department

Thus far we have examined only the budgetary knowledge of federal bureaucrats. State-level bureaucrats, however, may have higher knowledge of their agency's budget than do their federal counterparts. We postulated that it would be an easier enterprise for a state bureaucrat to be knowledgeable about their agency's budget than it would be for a federal bureaucrat following the more complicated machinations of the federal budgetary process. To examine this possibility, we studied the responses from our survey of the New Mexico Environment Department. The surveys were received from March through June of 1997. This period was near the end of the state's fiscal year 1997, which closed on June 30. In the five years preceding the questionnaire responses, from fiscal year 1993 through fiscal year 1997 (a period in which Governors Bruce King, a Democrat, and Gary Johnson, a Republican, were in charge), the NMED's actual budget increased from $28.931 million to $52.785 million, an increase of 82 percent unadjusted for inflation (Executive Budget Document, NM Department of Finance and Administration). The compounded rate of inflation during that same period, as measured by the consumer price index average for all measured goods and services, was 15 percent; the budget of the NMED therefore actually increased by 67 percent in real dollars during the period in question. How accurate were the estimates of NMED personnel regarding this state of affairs? Table 6.2 presents the range of responses to the questions. Some specific responses have been combined into ranges of response for ease of presentation.

While the range of responses was comparable to those of the EPA respondents, the inaccuracy of the impressions of the vast majority of NMED members is, to say the least, striking. Over half (53 percent) of those responding thought that the budget for the agency had actually decreased during the period in question. More than three-quarters of the respondents (77 percent) thought that the agency's budget had decreased by up to 30 percent. Only twenty-six respondents—one-fifth of the total group—correctly knew that the budget had in fact increased, and only two were close to the real figure. Of course such results speak loudly against the hypothesis that bureaucrats are generally knowledgeable about their agencies' budgets. Since the NMED sample, unlike its EPA counterpart, included administrative as well as technical personnel, dif-

Table 6.2
Estimated Levels of the NMED's Budget Increase or Decrease 1993–1997:
All Personnel (N = 128)

Estimated Level (%) + or −	Accuracy Score	Frequency	Valid Percent
−50	117	1	0.8
−40	107	1	0.8
−30	97	3	2.3
−20 to −29	87–96	14	11.0
−10 to −19	77–86	34	26.5
−1 to −9	68–76	15	11.8
0= stayed the same	67	36	28.1
1 to 10	57–66	9	7.1
11 to 20	47–56	10	7.8
21 to 29	38–46	3	2.4
30	37	2	1.6
50	17	1	0.8
67	**0**	**0**	**0.0**
72	5	1	0.8

Note: Bold = correct response.

ferences between these two groups were examined. The administrative personnel were slightly more accurate than were their technical coworkers in their directional assessments of variation in the budget; 48 percent of administrators/managers thought the budget had decreased, compared to 58 percent of the technical respondents who thought so.

Independent Variables and Budget Knowledge

The dependent variable used for the analyses of budget accuracy was a ratio-level measurement. In the case of the NMED, +67 (the correct answer to the question of the direction and the amount of change in the NMED budget over the previous five years—1993 through 1997) was set equal to zero and all other estimations were calculated relative to their distances from that point. The independent variables examined first were those inferred from the Niskanen framework to be related to a higher degree of budget knowledge.

Since the NMED sample does contain a substantial number of administrative members—thirty-seven of the one hundred twenty-three that answered (30 percent)—the analysis was able to differentiate between those administrative/managerial personnel predicted by the revised Niskanen model to have the greatest degree of budget knowledge and their technical coworkers. Of the 30 percent who had administrative or managerial duties, eight (22 percent of administrators) specifically had financial responsibilities. It is reasonable, according to the microeconomics-based framework, to expect that this subgroup would be the most budget-savvy of any agency personnel. Table 6.3 presents the accuracy of budget variation estimates according to job descriptions.

An initial examination of the table reveals little to indicate that financial or other managerial personnel are more accurate in their budget perceptions than their technical colleagues. On a scale of 0–117, where 0 is most accurate, no financial bureaucrat is in the top 50 percentile of accuracy regarding budget variation. In fact, no financial member achieves a score lower than the 61–70 zone in terms of accuracy. Of the technical subset, on the other hand, 17 percent achieved scores of 0–60, with 10 percent below 50. By this measure, the technical personnel hypothesized to be least knowledgeable about budget fluctuations are in fact the most knowledgeable of three groups. Overall difference of means-significance test results for the independent variables were included next but no statistically significant relationships overall were found between any of the independent variables predicted by the Niskanen thesis and accuracy of budget variance knowledge.

Contrary to basic assumptions of the Niskanen formulation, no significant difference in budget estimations were demonstrated by respondents who would or would not take jobs with other state agencies or with regulated industry. NMED bureaucrats do not seem to strongly

Table 6.3

Accuracy of Estimated Five-Year Budget Changes by Type of NMED Employee

Accuracy Score (0 = most accurate)	Financial Personnel (% of subset)	Administrative/ Managerial Personnel (% of subset)*	Technical Personnel (% of subset)*
0–40	0 (0)	0 (0)	4 (5)
41–50	0 (0)	3 (10)	4 (5)
51–60	0 (0)	1 (3)	6 (7)
61–70	5 (62.5)	10 (34)	26 (30)
70–80	1 (12.5)	10 (34)	23 (27)
81–90	1 (12.5)	5 (17)	17 (20)
91–117	1 (12.5)	0 (0)	6 (7)
Total	8 (100)	29 (100)	86 (100)

*Percentages rounded to nearest whole number.

identify their personal interests with those of the agency. Little institutional loyalty on the part of bureau members is reflected by the results. This conclusion is reinforced by the finding that those who would expect to benefit from a 10 percent budget-hike for the agency were no more accurate in their budget assessments than those who did not. The means between responses of the two groups were amazingly similar. The assertion that bureaucrats identify their rational self-interests with the bureau due to expectations of personal reward resulting from agency gain, or due to loyalty to the bureau borne of personal investment are simply not supported by these data.

The budget-maximizer framework predicts those respondents who did think NMED's enforcement behavior would influence sponsors' budget recommendations (*agree* responses) would be more knowledgeable about the budget. Yet, none of the responses from the NMED members regarding sponsors' budget recommendations were significantly related to budget knowledge. When asked whether they agree or disagree with the statements that the manner in which NMED enforces the law affects the budgetary recommendations of three sponsors included on the NMED survey instrument—the Legislature, the Johnson administration, and the DFA respectively—there were no overall significant relationships.

Personal Gain from Agency Budget Increases

Further analyses of questions regarding expectations of personal benefit showed that only 69 percent of the respondents said they would expect their offices to benefit from a 10 percent agency-wide budget increase. It will be recalled that the EPA members reported a nearly identical distribution of responses to this question. Bivariate analysis further showed no significant relationship between expectations of benefit from a 10 percent budget increase and the type of job, as specified above, the respondent held. Therefore, an employee is no more likely to be budget-savvy, or to expect personally to benefit from agency gains if he/she is a financial, managerial, or technical worker.[2]

In summary, while there is some scattered evidence in our results to support Niskanen's thesis (two-thirds of respondents in both surveys do see a benefit in an increase in their budget), the preponderance of the evidence does not support the basic assumptions of the Niskanen budget-maximization model. In both samples, knowledge of budget variation was low. As measured by estimates of direction of variation alone, the

EPA respondents (federal employees) were more accurate overall than their NMED (state) counterparts. The NMED respondents were extremely inaccurate in their estimates of budget patterns. Nearly 83 percent thought that the budget had decreased or remained the same, when in fact it had increased by 77 percent in the relevant time period. Interestingly, NMED financial managers not only failed to display any statistically significant difference from their non-financial and technical colleagues in terms of budget accuracy, but on average they were actually less accurate in their estimates than the other two groups. Given the larger sample of NMED personnel, and the more discerning categorization of their job types than was present in the federal sample, the Niskanen conclusion that managerial/supervisory members would be more budget-conscious than their technician coworkers is simply not empirically supportable.

We also conclude that expectations of personal benefit from agency budget increases are by no means universal. One-third of the respondents in both groups stated that they had no such expectation. Additionally, those who do expect such benefits are no more likely to have accurate budgetary perceptions than are those who do not. These findings undermine the basic budget-maximizer assumption that personal and bureau utility is perceived as the same thing.

In short, our strongest conclusion in support of the Niskanen thesis is that some bureaucrats may exhibit qualities that can be considered budget maximizing; as a result we can conceive of a category or type of budget-maximizing bureaucrat. On the other hand, we do find consistent evidence that the Niskanen thesis is not generalizable to all bureaucrats, or even to all management/supervisors.

7

The Myths of the Bureaucracy

At present the principal-agent model is the dominant theory of political control of the bureaucracy. The theory posits that there is inherent goal conflict between principals and their agents, and that agents possess and benefit from an information asymmetry over their principals. In this book we have used interviews with federal- and state-level environmental personnel to shed some empirical light on the model's two basic assumptions. After presenting a critique of the model in chapter 2, we provided evidence supporting the model's assumptions in chapter 4. The data derived from our surveys on the educational training of environmental personnel demonstrated that most of the EPA and NMED employees have considerable specialized training or expertise. In addition, we found that a large number of EPA enforcement personnel perceive themselves as exerting bureaucratic discretion across four of five different compliance or monitoring tasks. From the assumptions of the principal-agent model we can extrapolate that the more discretion bureaucrats have, the more capable they will be of using an information asymmetry to shirk principal attempts at overhead political control.

We also found evidence that there is goal conflict between principals and their agents. We found that EPA NPDES enforcement personnel perceived their congressional oversight committees as having less commitment to environmental regulation than the Clinton administration. Likewise, the NMED bureaucrats perceived little commitment to environmental regulation from New Mexico's governor, Gary Johnson.

These results indicate that there is indeed empirical support for the principal-agent model's two key assumptions. Therefore, we can identify evidence for both an information asymmetry and goal conflict. Once we move to a two-principal, one-agent model of political control, however, agents have an incentive to act strategically—to align themselves politically with a principal who most closely reflects their policy goals. In the case of EPA enforcement personnel, this would mean that they would have been wise to more firmly align themselves with members of the Clinton administration than their congressional oversight committees. For NMED bureaucrats, this would mean a closer political relationship with their state legislative oversight committees than with the governor. In short, once we move to a multiple principal situation, agents have strategic options that are not available in a dyadic principal-agent model, particularly in periods of divided government (see Hammond and Knott 1996). On the other hand, principals have yet another obstacle to political control of the bureaucracy: not only must they do battle with potentially recalcitrant bureaucrats, they also must deal with other principals who do not share their own policy goals.

This point is important because EPA and NMED agents do not merely deal with representatives of the executive and legislative branches. As we demonstrated in chapters 4 and 5, federal and state-level bureaucratic agents interact with a wide variety of principals. More importantly, they perceive a wide range of principals as exerting at least some level of influence over how their office enforces the law, including a number of principals rarely incorporated in principal-agent models. For example, agents in both the EPA and the NMED drew a distinction between presidential influence and the influence of presidential appointees (the EPA administrator and the ten EPA regional administrators). EPA personnel perceived the federal courts as exerting considerable influence. Other policy actors, including the public, the media, environmental groups, and business groups also were perceived as exerting influence. The data on contacts with NMED environmental personnel indicated an even wider array of interaction with political actors, both within government (e.g., sponsors such as elected or appointed officials) and outside of it (e.g., clients such as interest groups and the public).

Our analysis of multiple principal bureaucratic politics also suggests that agents may perceive different principals as exerting similar types of influence. In chapter 5 we called this coalition process the venues of influence. Consequently, agents have an incentive to treat different types of principals in different ways, such as responding more substantively to some principals and more symbolically to others.

In sum, while there is evidence that goal conflict and an information asymmetry exist, there also is evidence that agents interact with a wide variety of political principals. What are the implications of these findings for models of political control of the bureaucracy? First, as noted above, a multiple principal game would mean that agents would have incentives to be strategic political actors, moving toward those principals who best represent their policy preferences. Second, in this process, agents may have an incentive, at least selectively, to provide or leak information to one principal (or set of principals) in order to offset the negative effects of political control from another principal (or set of principals). Third, agents may even be encouraged to build coalitions with other agents who share similar goals and thus broadly share information. Hence, fourth, once we add multiple principals to the model, the political process begins to more closely resemble the assumptions of an advocacy coalition relationship rather than the traditional principal-agent model.

Our analysis also raises other issues. For example, a normative assumption of the principal-agent model is that political control by principals is desirable because they are elected and hence are more representative of the American public. This assumption is aided by the common perception that environmental protection bureaucrats are, by nature, more extreme in their attitudes toward the environment than the general population. In chapter 3, however, our survey of EPA and NMED bureaucrats found their political views to be balanced. They did not rate the environment more highly than other important issues (crime, the economy, etc.), nor did they identify their bureaucratic tasks (EPA and water policy) as being of predominant concern. Certainly, neither EPA nor NMED personnel could be described as environmental zealots; in many ways, then, the bureaucrats in the two agencies that we examined seemed quite representative of the views of the American public.

This is a significant point, for the principal-agent theory makes much of the fact that principals are elected and thus are representative while agents are not. But does a Congress that believes in abandoning long-held views on environmental protection (as did the Congress elected in 1994) or a president who ardently opposes the mission of the Environmental Protection Agency (as did Ronald Reagan in the 1980s) really *represent* the American public better than agency personnel who are given the task of enforcing existing environmental laws? Certainly, the answer to this question will vary from individual to individual. Our point here is that for many individuals, the EPA better represented their environmental attitudes than did the elected Republican Congress in 1994 or the elected president in 1980 and 1984. Thus, when we consider the concept of representation, we need to consider it in a multidimensional context. We should not simply think in terms of whether one official is elected while another is not. We also need to examine what these policy actors stand for and what policies they represent.

In addition to the principal-agent model, we also examined the assumptions of a second economic-based model of bureaucratic politics: Niskanen's budget-maximizing bureaucrat model. That model has been a mainstay of bureaucratic politics for the past three decades. In chapter 6 we provided an empirical test of some of the theory's assumptions. Niskanen posits that agents are utility-maximizers and that they are primarily concerned with maximizing their agency's budget. Since they are primarily concerned with budgetary outcomes, we would expect them to have a certain level of basic knowledge about their budget. Yet, when we asked them whether their agency's budget had increased, decreased, or stayed about the same over the past five years, few EPA or NMED personnel could correctly identify the revenue direction of their agency's budget and few agreed in their responses; even fewer agents could identify the actual level of change. Agents were then asked if they would benefit if the agency's budget were increased. While about 70 percent in each agency said yes, 30 percent said no. If a substantial number of bureaucrats (about one-third) do not perceive a direct benefit from budget increases, we believe that at least raises questions about a basic assumption of Niskanen's theory. The budget-maximizing bureaucrat may exist; it may be only one type of agent (see the Downs 1967 typology for other types of bureaucrats) and not the only one. Some agents likely are budget maximizers, while others likely are motivated by policy or other goals (see Brehm and Gates 1999).

Consequently, while our analysis provides some supportive evidence for two prominent theories of the bureaucratic process, we also raise questions about other assumptions. In particular, we recommend the development of theories that provide a more dynamic interaction between multiple principals, multiple agents, and agents motivated by a variety of goals. We are especially critical of theories that include normative bureaucrat-bashing assumptions (e.g., bureaucrats shirk, they do not represent the public interest, they are only interested in developing slack resources and increasing their budgets). Such assumptions, along with pejorative public portrayals of the bureaucracy have created what we call the myths of the bureaucracy, a set of often contradictory perceptions about the nature of bureaucrats and the bureaucratic process.

What are the Myths of the Bureaucracy?

One goal of this book is to reconcile some contradictions about the nature of the bureaucratic state that exist both within the public realm and within the scholarly literature. In preparation for this task, we examined a wide range of scholarly studies of the bureaucratic process. From these sources we compiled a list of twenty commonly advanced characteristics of the bureaucratic process, which we present as "myths" in the sections below. In general, the myths are highly pejorative. Often, the sole reason given for the existence of the bureaucracy is merely to perpetuate itself. Moreover, even a cursory analysis of the twenty myths listed in this chapter reveals the existence of major inconsistencies. For example, bureaucrats are perceived as possessing too much power and discretion, and as being out of control. At the same time, however, they are judged to be timid and incapable of getting anything done; the bureaucracy is seen as lumbering and resistant to change. Clearly, it is difficult to reconcile these generally perceived characteristics.

Politics and the Bureaucracy

The first two myths suggest that bureaucratic agents are not political actors.

1. There are no politics in administration.

2. Bureaucrats are policy-neutral.

The first myth is derived from the politics-administration dichotomy. In chapter 2, Waterman and Meier hypothesize that there are cases in which the assumptions of this dichotomy could exist: when there is goal consensus between principals and agents, and when agents possess a great deal of information while principals possess little information, the resulting politics will be indicative of the dichotomy. While the politics-administration dichotomy used to be considered by scholars as a broad description of the bureaucratic process, it is hypothesized that there can be cases in which no politics (or at least very little politics) exist in an administrative setting, but only when the aforementioned conditions exist. Therefore, we do not extend the dichotomy to a general theory of bureaucratic politics, as often has been done in the past. It is simply one possible outcome in the varied bureaucratic political world.

The same can be said for the second characteristic, the idea that bureaucrats are policy-neutral, an idea discussed by Heclo (1975) in his analysis of the Office of Management and Budget and his discussion of "neutral competence." In circumstances where goal consensus between principals and agents exist, and particularly in those cases where agents have little information, they are more likely to be policy-neutral. Neither the idea of a politics-administration dichotomy nor neutral competence in and of itself, then, is a myth. When, however, we extend this expectation to all bureaucrats in all political settings, it is not realistic. All bureaucrats are not policy-neutral. If, however, we limit it to those circumstances or cases where it is most likely to occur, then it provides further evidence of the diverse and dynamic nature of the bureaucratic process. Agents can be policy-neutral actors, but they also can exhibit traits of "responsive-competence" (see Moe 1985b). In short, specific, identifiable conditions determine if the policy neutrality of bureaucrats is myth or reality.

How Representative Is the Bureaucracy?

The next four commonly held perceptions show that, in general, the bureaucracy is not portrayed as at all representative or democratic.

3. Bureaucracy is an instrument of elite influence.

4. Bureaucracy is not an instrument of democracy.

5. Bureaucracy is unresponsive to citizen or public preferences.

6. Bureaucracy is unresponsive to the preferences of elected officials.

The third myth is derived from the capture theory and other writings. Bureaucracy can be an instrument of elite influence if we consider only elected officials as representing the public. In this circumstance, bureaucrats would represent the unelected elite while elected officials would represent the will of the people. This kind of thinking leads Lowi (1979) to argue that bureaucracy is not an instrument of democracy. Further evidence for this point is the fact that the bureaucracy is not identified in the Constitution. Yet the Constitution is silent on many matters. The Founders wanted to limit the influence of political parties, interest groups, and public opinion (the seeds of faction), so the existence of bureaucracy, like these other extra-constitutional political actors, should not in and of itself be considered undemocratic simply because it does not have a clear constitutional foundation.

In fact, for us to determine if bureaucracy is democratic or not we need to examine how responsive it is to the public and to elected officials (myths 5 and 6, argued by the capture theorists and much of the literature cited in chapter 3, respectively). Research over the past two decades has demonstrated empirically, we think beyond question, that agents do respond to such varied elected principals as the president and the Congress (see for example, Stewart and Cromartie 1982; Moe 1982; 1985a; 1985b; Wood and Waterman 1991). In addition, Krause (1999) has demonstrated that principals are responsive to agents. Hence, if we consider responsiveness to and by elected officials as evidence of democracy, then the empirical evidence indicates that the bureaucracy is indeed integrated into the democratic fabric of our nation, more so than research prior to the 1980s suggested.

Our own results, illustrated in chapters 4 and 5, also shed some light on this point. Bureaucrats working for state and federal agencies indicated that they perceived a wide array of principals as exerting influence over how their office enforced the law. Bureaucrats likely would not perceive such high levels of influence across policy actors if they were not responsive to them (or at least concerned about them) to some degree. NMED bureaucrats also reported a large number of contacts with various political actors. In short, while the question of whether the bureaucracy is democratic or not is clearly a normative one, and a more complete answer to that question is far beyond the scope of this book, we believe there is evidence that bureaucracy, at least potentially, can be a democratizing agent in our political system.

Passive Principals

Related to the notion of democratic agents is the question of whether elected officials have the ability to control the bureaucracy. As we noted in chapter 3, it has been long assumed that principals are passive and hence exhibit little influence over the bureaucracy. Thus, the following perceptions also have been commonly expressed in the bureaucratic literature.

7. The courts merely defer to the greater expertise of the bureaucracy.

8. Elected officials are outside of the bureaucratic policy loop.

9. Elected officials are not interested in overseeing or controlling the bureaucracy.

10. Even if they were interested, elected officials do not have the necessary political resources to exert effective influence over the bureaucracy.

For instance, it once was common wisdom that the courts merely deferred to the greater expertise of the bureaucracy. Much evidence can be provided to support this point if we examine the courts and their relationship to the bureaucracy in the period prior to the 1970s. Since that time, however, the courts have become much more active in overseeing the bureaucracy. Melnick (1983) documents the more activist interaction between the courts and the EPA with regard to the Clean Air Act of 1970; Moe (1985a) draws a connection between the influence of the courts and Federal Trade Commission's enforcement policies; and Wood and Waterman (1993) find a connection between fines issued by the courts and EPA enforcement behavior. Likewise, in chapter 4 of this book, we show that EPA officials perceive the federal courts as being one of the most influential policy actors. While the state courts are not seen as having as much influence (by state or federal officials) it is clear that the federal courts can no longer be described as merely deferring to the greater expertise of the bureaucracy.

The same can be said with regard to the Congress and the president. In our survey, EPA enforcement personnel also identified the Congress as exhibiting a great deal of influence over the bureaucracy. While they ranked presidential influence considerably lower, they did perceive high levels of influence by two types of presidential appointees, the EPA administrator, and the regional administrators. At the state level, agency personnel also perceived the governor, the state legislature, and their budgetary oversight mechanisms as exerting considerable influence, as well as the U.S. Congress.

Again, the basis for the idea that various principals cannot control the bureaucracy may be historical in nature. In the 1950s and 1960s, when this view was regularly espoused, presidents and Congress exhibited much less interest in bureaucratic oversight, and they often did not use their resources effectively to control agencies. At that time, however, bureaucratic politics was commonly described with reference to "agency capture" and the "iron triangle" theory. By the 1970s, however, the iron triangles were breaking up (Derthick and Quirk 1985) and a new breed of bureaucratic politics, one in which presidents, the Congress, and the courts played an activist role, was introduced (see Nathan 1983; Melnick 1983; Aberbach 1990). Legislation creating such social regulatory agencies as the EPA encouraged a more active oversight role for all three of these principals, and particularly for the courts. Furthermore, the deregulation movement pitted agencies against their regulated industries, with both the president and Congress playing more active policy-setting roles (see Waterman 1989). Therefore, while the assumptions expressed in myths 7–10 may have had greater validity in the past, today they are dated assumptions contradicted by a great deal of empirical evidence.

Power and the Bureaucracy

The questions of whether the bureaucracy is democratic and whether principals exert real oversight are key to understanding the next set of commonly assumed characteristics of the bureaucracy (see Lowi 1979).

11. Bureaucracy has too much power.

12. Bureaucrats possess too much discretion.

13. Bureaucracy lacks accountability.

14. Bureaucracy is out of control.

15. Bureaucracy is too political.

If no external political actor controlled the bureaucracy, then it would indeed have too much power. If the president, the Congress, or the courts could not control it, then bureaucracy would lack accountability to elected officials and the public at large. If it lacked accountability, then the bureaucracy would indeed be out of control. Furthermore, if principals did not have the resources to control the bureaucracy, then the bureaucracy also would be uncontrollable. Yet, as we have argued, there is considerable empirical evidence suggesting that these still commonly expressed assumptions are no longer valid. One can normatively argue that bureaucracy has too much power. One can argue that the power of the bureaucracy should be returned to the people or to the states. The movement toward the privatization of public functions is clearly an attempt to limit bureaucratic power. While the proper scope of bureaucratic power is a subject that even the authors of this book cannot agree upon, it is clear that the bureaucracy does not have unlimited power. Its power is bounded by the many factors we have identified in this book. Oversight by elected officials is possible and does occur. In addition, a wide variety of policy actors (both hierarchical and non-hierarchical) exert influence. Consequently, if the bureaucracy lacks accountability, it is possible for principals to remedy this problem. As much empirical evidence now shows, bureaucracy can be controlled. Again, whether it is as accountable as individuals desire or as controlled as politicians prefer is a normative question we cannot fully address here. Some people obviously would prefer a smaller bureaucracy, with more oversight by elected officials and even greater control by elected officials. Others, fearing the policy direction of conservative elected officials, would prefer to give more discretion to the bureaucracy. What we have argued, and what other research we have cited throughout this book demonstrates, is that such outcomes are possible. Principals can control the bureaucracy and limit bureaucratic power.

Does the bureaucracy have too much discretion, however? This is a point that has dominated the literature for many years. When bureaucratic discretion is mentioned, it is usually discussed as something that needs to be controlled and not as a positive attribute to be encouraged (e.g., Lowi 1979; though see Hunter and Waterman 1992). While the proper scope of bureaucratic discretion is a normative question, we have demonstrated that EPA NPDES personnel do perceive themselves as exerting it in various tasks they perform. Again, we argue that to generalize that all bureaucrats have too much discretion or are out of control is a myth. We do not expect the same level of discretion to exist in all agencies. Those that have agents with limited information should have less discretion than those in which agents possess considerable information.

Bureaucratic Personal Characteristics

The last five commonly expressed perceptions about the bureaucracy relate to the personal characteristics of bureaucrats and the resulting impact on bureaucratic politics. Many of these derive from campaign speeches, as well as from popular accounts of the bureaucracy by the media, literature, and film.

16. Bureaucrats are timid.

17. Bureaucrats can't get anything done.

18. Bureaucracy is a slow, lumbering giant.

19. Bureaucracy is static, and therefore not dynamic.

20. Bureaucracy is resistant to change.

What we find most interesting about the last five commonly held characteristics are the contradictions between them, much as Simon (1946) argued in his classic work that the then commonly accepted "proverbs of administration" were contradictory in many important respects. Scholars argue that there are no politics in administration, yet they also accuse bureaucrats of being too political. It is widely believed that bureaucrats are too timid and hence can't get anything done, yet it is also widely believed that the bureaucracy has too much power. When politicians in one breath accuse the bureaucracy of being power-mongers, then in the next attack bureaucrats for being ineffectual, they are presenting the public with a contradictory portrayal of the bureaucracy. Certainly there are bureaucrats who are timid, certainly there are agencies that cannot get anything done, and certainly there are agencies that have too much power. If we consider these views as possible outcomes they are not unreasonable. If, however, we consider them as generalizable descriptions of the bureaucracy, they are indeed conflicting and unreasonable. The same is true for other generalizations, such as that the bureaucracy is a large, lumbering giant or that it static and resistant to change. It is difficult to conceptualize power-mongers who are timid, resistant to change, static, and lumbering. Yet that is precisely the way the bureaucracy is commonly portrayed.

These twenty commonly held perceptions that we call the myths of the bureaucracy are not intended as a comprehensive list of all possible perceptions or misperceptions of bureaucracy, and hence we certainly do not believe that the discussion of bureaucratic politics should end here. Rather, what we have tried to do is to address more general concerns in the bureaucratic politics field and to provide some insights that may help us advance the discussion and debate on these issues.

Throughout this book we have argued that we need to reexamine the theories we use to explain bureaucratic politics. As we have found, there are iron triangle relationships, budget-maximizing bureaucrats, and agencies best explained as traditional principal-agent relationships. Yet, when we adopt absolute statements, we contribute to the creation of new myths of the bureaucracy. The tendency in the literature has been to make unqualified statements about bureaucracy as if it is one monolithic entity, alike everywhere that it can be found. In reality, there are myriad bureaucratic settings, and we need to begin to identify the characteristics of them so that we can develop more generalizable theories of the bureaucratic process.

APPENDIX

A Brief History of Water Pollution Legislation

The United States of America's water pollution legislation can be traced back to the Refuse Act of 1899.[1] The Refuse Act was created to address the problems of industrial effluents then affecting the navigability of the nation's waterways. Although the purpose of the Refuse Act was to increase maritime safety, the resultant permitting process also served as a means to improve water quality. The bill required the approval of the Army Corps of Engineers approval for any discharge and offered of a "bounty" to citizens who supplied information to the government to help enforce the permitting procedure. There were provisions for penalties for noncompliance but there were no guidelines for the granting or denial of permits.

Congress next passed the Water Pollution Control Act of 1948 (amended in 1956). This increased federal involvement in water quality issues by providing funds for construction and the operation of waste treatment plants. To further assist states in setting water quality standards, the Water Quality Act of 1965 was enacted. Even as the Clean Water Restoration Act of 1966 increased federal funding for state water programs, government officials were beginning to realize that the uneven manner in which water laws had been applied, largely the result of varying state standards, could not adequately address the nation's growing water pollution problems. Hence, during the late 1960s attention began to turn to a national solution to the nation's water problems.

Several factors common to water laws prior to 1970 had to be addressed in this next round of legislation. First, identification of point of discharge was difficult, creating a pattern of uneven regulation and punishment. Second, variance in state standards and a lack of accountability for shared waterways created a difficult regulatory environment for the nation's intrastate rivers and lakes. And third, most federal programs were hampered by requirements for state consent for enforcement activities. In the wake of the Clean Air Act of 1970 Congress's attempt to create an equivalent water bill, the 1970 Water Quality Improvement Act, succeeded only in creating a national policy for oil spills and the treatment of sewage from recreational boats. Summarizing seventy-one years of water laws, Arbuckle (1993, 151) writes, "In short, the process of protecting a designated quality of a receiving stream involved insurmountable technical and political challenges and was largely ineffectual."

In response to the increased public interest in environmental awareness in the early 1970s, President Richard Nixon revived the Refuse Act of 1899 for the purposes of water pollution abatement. For the first time, national standards for permits and fines for noncompliance were viable tools for regulating water quality. The 1970 reincarnation of the 1899 Refuse Act, however, posed several problems for 'modern' enforcement: there were no standards for the granting or denial of discharge permits; the fines for noncompliance were considered inadequate; there was some overlap with the National Environmental Policy Act's (1969) requirement of Environmental Impact Statements; and the relationship of the Refuse Act to other environmental legislation was unclear (Arbuckle 1993).

The Federal Water Pollution Control Act (FWPCA) of 1972 was offered as the legislative solution to the uneven and ineffective water protection programs of the past. Passed by Congress over Nixon's veto, the FWPCA became familiarly known as the Clean Water Act (CWA) whose stated objective was: "to restore and maintain the chemical, physical and biological integrity of the nation's waters" (Arbuckle 1993, 155). The act's basic goal was to regulate every pollutant or contaminant discharged by facilities into the nation's waters.

The cornerstone of the CWA was the creation of the National Pollutant Discharge Elimination System (NPDES) as the permitting and enforcement body for some sixty thousand conditional authorizations to discharge. Industry-by-industry standards were to be set based on the best available pollution control technology, with consideration given to the cost of implementation to the regulated industries. Industries were required to apply for discharge permits and to confirm compliance and report noncompliance to the sovereign agency. NPDES monitoring and reporting functions (whether EPA- or state-controlled) include: creation and enforcement of compliance schedules, setting effluent limitations, re-permitting, and permit revocation. Enforcement tools available under the NPDES range from warning letters to criminal lawsuits.

The responsibility for the development and enforcement of nation-wide water quality standards was assigned to the nascent Environmental Protection Agency. The CWA also created a means by which, under specified circumstances, states could take control of permitting and enforcement tasks. In these primacy states the EPA acts in an oversight capacity.

NOTES

2. Principal-Agent Models: A Theoretical Cul-de-Sac

Waterman and Meier presented a version of this chapter at the Midwest Political Science Association, Chicago, Illinois, in April 1995. That paper was then substantially revised and published in the *Journal of Public Administration Research and Theory* (1998). In this chapter we are presenting a slightly altered version of the original Midwest paper.

1. These are clearly continuous variables. We dichotomize them only to simplify the presentation.

2. The arguments applied here to goal conflict also apply to conflict over means as well.

3. Other scholars adopted the related issue network and advocacy coalition frameworks as an extension of the iron triangle approach.

4. A second extremely interesting set of cases that is not discussed in the literature relate to the various notions of democracy. Responsiveness to a congressional committee is responsiveness to a different aspect of democracy than responsiveness to the entire Congress or to the presidency. Similarly responsiveness to clientele is different still. There are major issues concerning how responsive some of the relationships are to majoritarian notions of democracy (see Redford 1969; Meier 1993). With multiple principals, bureaucratic relationships must be examined in their full environment to avoid a misleading perception.

5. This is limit of the applications, not a limit of the models. The true principal-agent model is a competitive game. Both the principal and the agent can influence the behavior of the other. Both must consider the actions of the other in any strategies that they undertake.

6. This conflict between individual goals and organization goals is the heart of management as a field of study (see Barnard 1938).

3. The Nature of Bureaucratic Politics

1. See also Mete 2002.

2. Polls of the public about their political attitudes using liberal/conservative labels are notoriously problematic. There is a great deal of inconsistency in operationalization and measurement between polls, and polls are often internally

inconsistent in their results (Ladd 1994). Comparison of the data gathered here, therefore, of bureaucrats' ideological preferences with those of the general public must be done with a great deal of caution. Most polls, for example, use some version of three-point liberal-moderate-conservative scale, rather than the seven-point scale used in the surveys of the bureaucrats for this work. Also, the majority of polls of the general public ask about political attitudes in general, rather than making a distinction between social and economic issues as was done on the EPA and NMED surveys. Ladd (1994) has done extensive work in this area. His data are in general agreement with the CBS News / New York Times poll (see Wilson and DiIulio 1998), which also uses a three-point scale and asks about general political attitudes. The CBS News / New York Times poll was used here for comparison here because it was the most widely cited in the sources consulted.

3. This is from the 1994 data of the Inter-university Consortium for Political and Social Research (ICPSR) American National Election Studies at the University of Michigan.

4. An Examination of the Assumptions of the Principal-Agent Model

1. There is a vast literature dealing with bureaucratic discretion. For more on this subject see Kaufman 1960; Wilson 1968, 1980; Davis 1969a, 1969b; Lipsky 1971, 1980; Kaufman and Couzens 1973; Yin and Yates 1975; Britnall 1981; Worden 1984; Hedge, Menzel, and Krause 1989; Stevenson 1990; Epstein and O'Halloran 1994, 1999; Hunter and Waterman 1996; Kiewiet and McCubbins 1991; Huber and Shipan 2000, 2002; Meier and Bohte 2001.

2. Discretion also has impact on policy outcomes. As Meier and Bohte (2001) and Meier, Wrinkle, and Polinard (1999) show, higher levels of student performance are associated with greater levels of minority teacher discretion (though see Nielsen and Wolf 2001 for another view).

3. Is this discretion justifiable? On this point, there are those who advocate a less discretionary enforced compliance approach to environmental regulation (Freeman and Haveman 1972; Viscusi and Zechhauser 1979; Keiser 1980). This enforcement style is predicated on strict enforcement of the law and limited bureaucratic discretion as the most even-handed and effective means of protecting the environment. Bardach and Kagan (1982), however, suggest that to follow the letter of the law creates a climate of "regulatory unreasonableness" and suggests that EPA personnel be granted greater discretion to enforce the spirit of the law through negotiated compliance with the permittee. Hunter and Waterman (1992, 1996) find a "pragmatic enforcement" style prevalent in the enforcement of NPDES regulations. This regulatory approach is one in which adherence to the letter of the law is tempered by what is needed to produce the desired results. This latitude in enforcement discretion is recognized by the regulated community as well. In his text, *Environmental Law Handbook*, Arbuckle

instructs readers that NPDES requirements "can be the subject of negotiations. Accordingly, pollution control managers should determine the areas in which the act and regulations leave room for negotiation and, based on a careful assessment of the company's long-term interests, should negotiate actively in an effort to obtain favorable permit terms and conditions" (1993: 218).

4. We also chose these actions because monitoring the changes in the numbers of bureaucratic outputs is the methodology of top-down studies of bureaucratic behavior. For example, Wood (1988) used enforcement actions to study the responsiveness of the EPA to several Reagan-era interventions; Hedge and Scicchitano (1994) examined the oversight decisions of the Office of Surface Mining (OSM) to analyze the effects of federal and local political climates; and Britnall (1981) studied the effects of caseload on court and agency outcomes at the Consumer Protection Agency (see also Wilson 1968; Worden 1984; Meier, Stewart, and England 1991; Wood and Waterman 1991, 1993, 1994; Clark-Daniels and Daniels 1995; Hunter and Waterman, 1996).

5. The reason we have different percentages for the same number of responses is that some people only ranked the number one problem and did not proceed to identify the number 2 problem.

5. A Multiple Principal Model of Bureaucratic Politics

We would like to thank the Institute for Public Policy at the University of New Mexico for providing funding for an earlier version of chapter 5. An earlier version also was published in the *Journal of Public Administration Research and Theory* (1998).

1. For a discussion of the differences between purposive and material interest groups see Wilson (1973) and Salisbury (1969).

6. Bureaucrats' Knowledge of Their Budgets

1. For all subsequent analysis the value of an accurate prediction was set to zero and all other values were likewise adjusted.

2. We also examined the relationship of various demographic factors and budgetary knowledge. Only one factor was significant at the .05 level or lower: the bureaucrat's racial/ethnic background, though we have no clear theoretical explanation for why this is the case.

Appendix

1. 33 U.S.C. Section 407

REFERENCES

Aberbach, Joel D. 1990. *Keeping a Watchful Eye: The Politics of Congressional Oversight*. Washington, D.C.: Brookings Institution.

Aberbach, Joel D., Ellis S. Krauss, Michio Muramatsu, and Bert A. Rockman. 1990. "Comparing Japanese and American Administrative Elites." *British Journal of Political Science*. 20:461–488.

Aberbach, Joel D., Robert D. Putnam, and Bert A. Rockman. 1981. *Bureaucrats and Politicians in Western Democracies*. Cambridge, Mass.: Harvard University Press.

Aberbach, Joel D., and Bert A. Rockman. 1976. "Clashing Beliefs within the Executive Branch." *The American Political Science Review* 70:456–67.

———. 1990. "What Has Happened to the U.S. Senior Civil Service?" *Brookings Review* 8:35–41.

———. 1995. "The Political View of U.S. Senior Federal Executives, 1970–1992." *Journal of Politics* 57:838–52.

Aberbach, Joel D., Bert A. Rockman, and Robert M. Copeland. 1990. "From Nixon's Problem to Reagan's Achievement: The Federal Executive Reexamined." Pp. 175–94 in *Looking Back on the Reagan Presidency*, edited by Larry Berman. Baltimore: John Hopkins University Press.

Appleby, Paul. 1945. *Big Democracy*. New York: Alfred A. Knopf, Inc.

Arbuckle, Gordon J. 1993. *Environmental Law Handbook*. Twelfth Edition. Rockville: Government Institutes, Inc.

Babbie, Earl. 1990. *Survey Research Methods*. Belmont: Wadsworth Publishing Company.

Balla, Steven J. 1998. "Administrative Procedures and Political Control of the Bureaucracy." *American Political Science Review* 92:663–73.

Balla, Steven J., and John R. Wright. 2001. "Interest Groups, Advisory Committees, and Congressional Control of the Bureaucracy." *American Journal of Political Science* 45:799–812.

Banks, Jeffrey S. 1989. "Agency, Budgets, Cost Information, and Auditing." *American Journal of Political Science* 33:670–99.

Banks, Jeffrey S., and Barry R. Weingast. 1992. "The Political Control of Bureaucrats under Asymmetric Information." *American Journal of Political Science* 36:509–24.

Bardach, Eugene, and Robert A. Kagan. 1982. *Going by the Book, The Problem of Regulatory Unreasonableness*. Philadelphia: Temple University Press.

Barnard, Chester. 1938. *Functions of the Executive*. Cambridge, Mass.: Harvard University Press.

Barth, Thomas J. 1993. Constitutional Subordinate Autonomy: Serving Multiple Masters—A Normative Theory in Practice. *Administration & Society* 25:160–82.

Bawn, Kathleen. 1995. Political Control versus Expertise: Congressional Choices about Administrative Procedures. *American Political Science Review* 89:62–73.

Bendor, Jonathan, and Terry M. Moe. 1985. An Adaptive Model of Bureaucratic Politics. *American Political Science Review* 79:755–74.

Bendor, Jonathan, and D. Mookherjee. 1987. "Institutional Structure and the Logic of Ongoing Collective Action." *American Political Science Review* 81:129–54.

Bendor, Jonathan, Serge Taylor, and Roland Van Gaalen. 1985. "Bureaucratic Expertise vs. Legislative Authority." *American Political Science Review* 79:1041–60.

———. 1987. "Politicians, Bureaucrats, and Asymmetric Information." *American Journal of Political Science* 31:796–828.

Bernstein, Marver. 1955. *Regulating Business Through Independent Commission*. Princeton: Princeton University Press.

Bickers, Kenneth N., and Robert M. Stein. 1994. "A Portfolio Theory of Policy Subsystems." *Administration & Society* 26:158–84.

Blais, Andre, and Stephane Dion, eds. 1991. *The Budget-Maximizing Bureaucrat: Appraisals and Evidence*. Pittsburgh: University of Pittsburgh Press.

Bowman, Ann O'M. 1984. "Intergovernmental and Intersectoral Tensions in Environmental Policy Implementation." *Policy Studies Review* 4:230–44.

———. 1985a. "Hazardous Waste Cleanup and Superfund Implementation in the Southeast." *Policy Studies Journal* 14:100–110.

———. 1985b. "Hazardous Waste Management: An Emerging Policy within an Emerging Federalism." *Publius* 15:131–44.

Boyer, William W. 1964. *Bureaucracy on Trial: Policy Making by Government Agencies*. New York: Bobbs-Merrill.

Brehm, John, and Scott Gates. 1993. "Donut Shops and Speed Traps: Evaluating Models of Supervision of Police Behavior." *American Journal of Political Science* 27:555–81.

———. 1999. *Working, Shirking, and Sabotage: Bureaucratic Response to a Democratic Public*. Ann Arbor: University of Michigan Press.

Britnall, Michael. 1981. "Caseloads, Performance, and Street-Level Bureaucracy." *Urban Affairs Quarterly* 16:281–98.

Browne, William P. 1988. *Private Interests, Public Policy, and American Agriculture*. Lawrence, Kans.: University Press of Kansas.

Browne, William P., Jerry R. Skees, Louis E. Swanson, Paul B. Thompson, and Laurian J. Unnevehr. 1992. *Sacred Cows and Hot Potatoes: Agrarian Myths in Agricultural Policy.* Boulder, Colo.: Westview Press.

Brudney, Jeffrey L., and F. Ted Herbert. 1987. "State Agencies and Their Environments: Examining the Influence of Important External Actors." *Journal of Politics* 49:186–206.

Bryner, Gary C. 1987. *Bureaucratic Discretion: Law and Politics in Federal Regulatory Agencies.* New York: Pergamon Press.

Bullock, Charles S., III, and Joseph Stewart, Jr., 1984. "New Programs in 'Old' Agencies: Lessons in Organizational Change from the Office of Civil Rights." *Administration and Society* 15:387–412.

Calvert, Randall L., Matthew McCubbins, and Barry Weingast. 1989. "A Theory of Political Control and Agency Discretion." *American Journal of Political Science* 33:588–611.

Calvert, Randall, Mark J. Moran, and Barry R. Weingast. 1987. "Congressional Influence over Policymaking: The Case of the FTC." In *Congress: Structure and Policy,* edited by Matthew D. McCubbins and Terry Sullivan. New York: Cambridge University Press.

Carpenter, Daniel P. 1996. "Adaptive Signal Processing, Hierarchy, and Budgetary Control in Federal Regulation." *American Political Science Review* 90:283–302.

———. 2002. "Groups, the Media, Agency Waiting Costs, and FDA Drug Approval." *American Journal of Political Science* 46:490–505.

Cater, Douglas. 1964. *Power in Washington: A Critical Look at Today's Struggle to Govern in the Nation's Capitol.* New York: Random House.

Cheng, Joseph L. C. 1983. "Toward an Integration of Organization Research and Practice: A Contingency Study of Bureaucratic Control and Performance in Scientific Settings." *Administrative Science Quarterly* 28:85–100.

Clarke-Daniels, Carolyn L., and R. Steven Daniels. 1995. "Street-Level Decision Making in Elder Mistreatment Policy: An Empirical Case Study of Service Rationing." *Social Science Quarterly* 76:460–73.

Clay, Joy A. 1994. "Public-Institutional Processes: Beyond Conventional Wisdom about Management Processes." *Administration & Society* 26:236–51.

Cohen, Jeffrey E. 1985. "Presidential Control of Independent Regulatory Commissions through Appointment: The Case of the FCC." *Administration and Society* 17:61–70.

Cole Richard L., and David A. Caputo. 1979. "Presidential Control of the Senior Executive Service: Assessing Strategies for the Nixon Years." *American Political Science Review* 73:409–32.

Conybeare, John A. 1984. "Bureaucracy, Monopoly, and Competition: A Critical Analysis of the Budget-Maximizing Model of Bureaucracy." *American Journal of Political Science* 28:479–502.

Cook, Brian J. 1992. "The Representative Function of Bureaucracy." *Administration & Society* 23:403–29.

Cronin, Thomas E. 1980. *The State of the Presidency.* Boston: Little, Brown.

Davis, Kenneth Culp. 1969a. *Discretionary Justice: A Preliminary Inquiry.* Baton Rouge: Louisiana State University.

———. 1969b. "A New Approach to Delegation." *University of Chicago Law Review* 36:713–25.

Derthick, Martha, and Paul J. Quirk. 1985. *The Politics of Deregulation.* Washington, D.C.: Brookings Institution.

Dillman, Don A. 1978. *Mail and Telephone Surveys: The Total Design Method.* New York: John Wiley and Sons.

Dodd, Lawrence, C., and Richard L. Schott. 1979. *Congress and the Administrative State.* New York: John Wiley and Sons.

Downs, Anthony. 1967. *Inside Bureaucracy.* Boston: Little, Brown.

Downs, George W., and David M. Rocke. 1994. "Conflict, Agency, and Gambling for Resurrection: The Principal-Agent Problem Goes to War." *American Journal of Political Science* 38:362–80.

Eisner, Marc Allen. 1992. *Antitrust and the Triumph of Economics.* Chapel Hill: University of North Carolina Press.

Eisner, Marc Allen, and Kenneth J. Meier. 1990. "Presidential Control versus Bureaucratic Power: Explaining the Reagan Revolution in Antitrust." *American Journal of Political Science* 34:269–87.

Epstein, David, and Sharyn O'Halloran. 1994. "Administrative Procedures, Information and Agency Discretion." *American Journal of Political Science* 38:697–722.

———. 1996. "Divided Government and the Design of Administrative Procedures: A Formal Model and Empirical Test." *The Journal of Politics* 58:373–97.

———. 1999. *Delegating Powers: A Transaction Cost Politics Approach to Public Policy Making Under Separate Powers.* Cambridge: Cambridge University Press.

Erikson, Robert S., John P. McIver, and Gerald C. Wright, Jr. 1987. "State Political Culture and Public Opinion." *American Political Science Review* 81:797–813.

Evans, Robert G. 1980. "Professionals and the Production Function." In *Occupational Licensing and Regulation,* edited by Simon Rottenberg. Washington, D.C.: American Enterprise Institute.

Fellmuth, Robert C. 1970. *The Interstate Commerce Omission.* New York: Grossman.

Ferejohn, John A., and Charles R. Shipan. 1989. "Congressional Influence on Administrative Agencies: A Case Study of Telecommunications Policy. In *Congress Reconsidered,* edited by Lawrence C. Dodd and Bruce I. Oppenheimer. Washington, D.C.: Congressional Quarterly Press.

Fiorina, Morris. 1981. "Congressional Control of the Bureaucracy: A Mismatch of Incentives and Capabilities." In *Congress Reconsidered,* edited by Lawrence C.

Dodd and Bruce I. Oppenheimer. Washington, D.C.: Congressional Quarterly Press.

Foster, John L. 1990. "Bureaucratic Rigidity Revisited." *Social Science Quarterly* 71:223–38.

Fox, Richard, M. R. Crask, and K. Jonghoon. 1988. "Mail Survey Response Rate: A Meta-Analysis of Selected Techniques for Inducing Response." *Public Opinion Quarterly* 52: 467–91.

Freeman, A. Myrick, and Robert Haveman. 1972. "Clean Rhetoric and Dirty Water." *The Public Interest* 28:51–65.

Freeman, J. Leiper. 1965. *The Political Process*. New York: Random House.

Furlong, Scott R. 1998. "Political Influence on the Bureaucracy: The Bureaucracy Speaks." *Journal of Public Administration Research and Theory* 8:39–65.

Galloway, George B. 1951. "The Operation of the Legislative Reorganization Act of 1946." *American Political Science Review* 45:41–68.

Gergen, David. 2000. *Eyewitness to Power: The Essence of Leadership*. New York: Simon and Schuster.

Goodsell, Charles T. 1983. *The Case for Bureaucracy: A Public Administration Polemic*. Chatham, N.J.: Chatham House.

Gormley, William T. 1986. "Regulatory Issue Networks in a Federal System." *Policy* 18:595–620.

———. 1987. "Intergovernmental Conflict on Environmental Policy: The Attitudinal Connection." *Western Political Quarterly* 40:285–303.

———. 1989. *Taming the Bureaucracy: Muscles, Prayers, and Other Strategies*. Princeton: Princeton University Press.

Greenberg, Stanley B. 1995. *Middle Class Dreams: The Politics and Power of the New American Majority*. New York: Random House.

Grossman, Sanford J., and Oliver D. Hart. 1983. "An Analysis of the Principal-Agent Problem." *Econometrics* 51:7–45.

Hammond, Thomas H. 1986. "Agenda Control, Organizational Structure, and Bureaucratic Politics." *American Journal of Political Science* 30:379–419.

Hammond, Thomas H., and Jack H. Knott. 1996. "Who Controls the Bureaucracy? Presidential Power, Congressional Dominance, Legal Constraints, and Bureaucratic Autonomy in a Model of Multi-Institutional Policymaking." *Journal of Law, Economics, and Organization* 12:119–66.

Hammond, Thomas H., and Gary J. Miller. 1985. "A Social Choice Perspective on Authority and Expertise in Bureaucracy." *American Journal of Political Science* 29:1–28.

Hansen, Wendy. 1990. "The International Trade Commission and the Politics of Protectionism." *American Political Science Review* 84:21–43.

Hartwig, Richard. 1990. "The Paradox of Malevolent/Benevolent Bureaucracy." *Administration & Society* 22: 206–27.

Hasenfeld, Yeheskel, and Thomas Brock. 1991. "Implementation of Social Policy Re-Visited." *Administration & Society* 22:451–79.

Heclo, Hugh. 1975. "OMB and the Presidency—The Problems of Neutral Competence." *Public Interest* 38:80–98.

———. 1977. *A Government of Strangers: Executive Politics in Washington.* Washington, D.C.: Brookings Institution.

———. 1978. "Issue Networks and the Executive Establishment." In *The New American Political System,* edited by Anthony A. King. Washington, D.C.: American Enterprise Institute.

Hedge, David, M., Donald C. Menzel, and Mark A. Krause. 1989. "The Intergovernmental Milieu and Street-Level Implementation." *Social Science Quarterly* 70:285–99.

Hedge, David, M., and Michael J. Scicchitano. 1994. "Regulating in Space and Time: The Case of Regulatory Federalism." *Journal of Politics* 56:134–58.

Hedge, David, M., Michael J. Scicchitano, and Particia Metz. 1991. "The Principal-Agent Model and Regulatory Federalism." *The Western Political Quarterly* 44:1053–80.

Herring, Pendelton. 1967. *Public Administration and the Pubic Interest.* New York: Russell and Russell.

Hill, Larry B. 1989. "Refusing to Take Bureaucracy Seriously." Paper presented at the annual meeting of the Midwest Political Science Association, Chicago.

———. 1991. "Who Governs the American Administrative State? A Bureaucratic Centered Image of Government." *Journal of Public Administration Research and Theory.* 1:261–94.

Hill, Larry B., Gary Wamsley, and Charles T. Goodsell. 1992. *The State of Public Bureaucracy: Bureaucracies, Public Administration, and Public Policy.* Armonk, N.Y.: M. E. Sharpe.

Hindera, John J. 1993. "Representative Bureaucracy: Imprimis Evidence of Active Representation in the EEOC District Offices." *Social Science Quarterly* 74:95–108.

Hosseini, Hamshid C. and Robert L Armacost. 1993. "Gathering Sensitive Data in Organizations." *American Behavioral Scientist* 36:443–71.

Hubbell, Larry. 1992. "Four Archetypal Shadows: A Look at the Dark Side of Public Organizations." *Administration & Society* 24:205–23.

Huber, John, and Charles R. Shipan. 2000. "The Costs of Control: Legislators, Agencies, and Transaction Costs." *Legislative Studies Quarterly* 25:25–52.

———. 2002. *Deliberate Discretion? The Institutional Foundations of Bureaucratic Autonomy.* New York: Cambridge University Press.

Huber, John, Charles R. Shipan, and Madelaine Pfahler. 2001. "Legislatures and Statutory Control of Bureaucracy." *American Journal of Political Science* 45:330–345.

Hunter, Susan, and Richard W. Waterman. 1992. "Determining an Agency's Regulatory Style: How Does the EPA Water Office Enforce the Law?" *Western Political Quarterly.* 45:401–17.

———. 1996. *Enforcing the Law: The Case of the Clean Water Acts.* Armonk, N.Y.: M. E. Sharpe.

Huntington, Samuel P. 1952. "The Marasmus of the ICC: The Commission, the Railroads, and the Public Interest." *Yale Law Journal* 61:467–509.

Jenkins-Smith, Hank C. 1990. *Democratic Politics and Policy Analysis.* Pacific Grove: Brooks/Cole Publishing Company.

Jenkins-Smith, Hank C., Gilbert K. St. Clair, and Brian Woods. 1991. "Explaining Change in Policy Subsystems: Analysis of Coalition Stability and Defection Over Time." *American Journal of Political Science* 35:851–80.

Johnson, Cathy M. 1993. *The Dynamics of Conflict between Bureaucrats and Legislators.* Armonk, N.Y.: M. E. Sharpe.

Kaufman, Herbert. 1960. *The Forest Ranger. A Study in Administrative Behavior.* Baltimore: The Johns Hopkins University Press.

———. 1976. *Are Government Organizations Immortal?* Washington, D.C.: Brookings Institution.

———. 1981. *The Administrative Behavior of Federal Bureau Chiefs.* Washington, D.C.: Brookings Institution.

Kaufman, Herbert, and Michael Couzens. 1973. *Administrative Feedback, Monitoring Subordinates Behavior.* Washington, D.C.: Brookings Institution.

Keiser, Robert K. 1980. "The New Regulation of Health and Safety." *Political Science Quarterly* 95: 479–91.

Kelman, Steven. 1980. "Occupational Safety and Health Administration." Pp. 236–66 in *The Politics of Regulation,* edited by James Q. Wilson. New York: Basic Books.

Khademian, Anne M. 1995. "Reinventing a Government Corporation: Professional Priorities and a Clear Bottom Line." *Public Administration Review* (January/February).

Kiewiet, D. Roderick, and Mathew D. McCubbins. 1991. *The Logic of Delegation: Congressional and Parties and the Appropriations Process.* Chicago: University of Chicago Press.

Koenig, Louis. 1975. *The Chief Executive.* New York: Harcourt Brace Jovanovich.

Krause, George A. 1994. "Federal Reserve Policy Decision Making: Political and Bureaucratic Influences." *American Journal of Political Science* 38:124–44.

———. 1999. *A Two-Way Street: The Institutional Dynamics of the Modern Administrative State.* Pittsburgh: University of Pittsburgh Press.

Ladd, Everett C. 1994. "A New View of the Electorate." *American Enterprise* 5/6.

Landy, Mark K., Marc J. Roberts, and Stephen R. Thomas. 1994. *The Environmental Protection Agency: Asking the Wrong Questions from Nixon to Clinton*. New York: Oxford University Press.

Lester, James P. 1986. "New Federalism and Environmental Policy." *Publius: The Journal of Federalism* 16:149–65.

Lewis, David E. 2003. *Presidents and the Politics of Agency Design: Political Insulation in the United States Government Bureaucracy, 1946–1997*. Palo Alto, Calif.: Stanford University Press.

Lipsky, Michael. 1971. "Street-Level Bureaucracy and the Analysis of Urban Reform." *Urban Affairs Quarterly* 6:391–409.

———. 1980. *Street-Level Bureaucracy*. New York: Russell Sage Foundation.

Long, Norton E. 1949. "Power and Administration." *Public Administration Review* 9:257–64.

Lowery, David. 1993. "A Bureaucratic-Centered Image of Governance: The Founders' Thought in Modern Perspective." *Journal of Public Administration Research and Theory* 3:182–208.

Lowi, Theodore. 1979. *The End of Liberalism*. New York: Norton.

MacAvoy, Paul W. 1979. *The Regulated Industries and the Economy*. New York: Norton.

Mackay, Robert J., James C. Miller, III, and Bruce Yandle. 1987. *Public Choice and Regulation*. Stanford: The Hoover Institution.

Magat, Wesley A., Alan J. Krupnick, and Winston Harrington. 1986. *Rules in the Making: A Statistical Analysis of Regulatory Agency Behavior*. Washington, D.C.: Resources for the Future.

Mazmanian, Daniel A., and Jeanne Neinaber. 1979. *Can Organizations Change: Environmental Protection, Citizen Participation, and the Corps of Engineers*. Washington, D.C.: Brookings Institution.

Mazmanian, Daniel A., and Paul A. Sabatier. 1983. *Implementation and Public Policy*. Glenview, Ill.: Scott, Foresman.

McConnell, Grant. 1966. *Private Power and American Democracy*. New York: Knopf.

McCubbins, Mathew D. 1985. "The Legislative Design of Regulatory Structure." *American Journal of Political Science* 38: 124–44.

McCubbins, Mathew D., Roger Noll, and Barry Weingast. 1987. "Administrative Procedures as Instruments of Political Control." *Journal of Law, Economics, and Organization* 3:243–77.

———. 1989. "Structure and Process as Solutions to the Politician's Principal Agency Problem." "Structure and Process as Solutions to the Politician's Principal Agency Problem." *Virginia Law Review* 74:431–82.

McCubbins, Mathew D., and Thomas Schwartz. 1984. "Congressional Oversight Overlooked: Police Patrols Versus Fire Alarms." *American Journal of Political Science* 28:165–79.

Meier, Kenneth J. 1979. *Politics and the Bureaucracy. Policy-making in the Fourth Branch of Government*. North Scituate: Duxbury Press.

———.1988. *The Political Economy of Regulation: The Case of Insurance*. Albany: State University of New York Press.

———. 1993. *Politics and the Bureaucracy*. 3rd ed. Monterey, Calif.: Brooks/Cole.

———. 1994. *The Politics of Sin: Drugs, Alcohol and Public Policy*. Armonk, N.Y.: M. E. Sharpe.

Meier, Kenneth J., and John Bohte. 2001. "Structure and Discretion: Missing Links in Representative Bureaucracy." *Journal of Public Administration Research and Theory*. 11:455–70.

Meier, Kenneth J., J. L. Polinard, and Robert D. Wrinkle. 2000. "Bureaucracy and Organizational Performance: Causality Arguments about Public Schools." *American Journal of Political Science* 44:590–602.

Meier, Kenneth J., Joseph Stewart, and Robert E. England. 1991. "The Politics of Bureaucratic Discretion: Educational Access as an Urban Service." *American Journal of Political Science* 35:155–77.

Meier, Kenneth J., Robert Wrinkle, and J. L. Polinard. 1993. "Principal Agents and County Agents: Politics, Bureaucracy and Agriculture Policy." Paper presented at the annual meeting of the Midwest Political Science Association, Chicago.

———. 1994. "Buying the Farm: The Politics of Farm Credit." Paper presented at the annual meeting of the American Political Science Association, New York.

———. 1999. "Representative Bureaucracy and Distributional Equity: Addressing the Hard Questions." *Journal of Politics* 61:1025–39.

Melnick, R. Shep. 1983. *Regulations and the Courts: The Case of the Clean Air Act*. Washington, D.C.: Brookings Institution.

Mete, Mihriye. 2002. "Bureaucratic Behavior in Strategic Environments: Politicians, Taxpayers, and the IRS." *Journal of Politics*. 64:384–407.

Miller, Gary, and Terry M. Moe. 1983. "Bureaucrats, Legislators, and the Size of Government." *American Political Science Review* 77:297–322.

Mitnick, Barry M. 1980. *The Political Economy of Regulation*. New York: Columbia University Press.

Moe, Terry M. 1982. "Regulatory Performance and Presidential Administration." *American Journal of Political Science* 26:197–224.

———. 1984. "The New Economics of Organization." *American Journal of Political Science* 28:739–77.

———. 1985a. "Control and Feedback in Economic Regulation: The Case of the NLRB." *American Political Science Review* 79:1094–17.

———. 1985b. "The Politicized Presidency." Pp. 235–71 in *The New Directions in American Politics,* edited by John E. Chubb and Paul E. Peterson. Washington, D.C.: Brookings Institution.

———. 1987. "An Assessment of the Positive Theory of 'Congressional Dominance'." *Legislative Studies Quarterly* 12:475–520.

Moynihan, Daniel P. 1969. *Maximum Feasible Misunderstanding: Community Action in the War on Poverty*. New York: The Free Press.

Nathan, Richard P. 1983. *The Administrative Presidency*. New York: John Wiley and Sons.

New Mexico Environment Department Home Page. 2003. <http://www.nmenv.state.nm.us/>.

Nielsen, Laura B., and Patrick J. Wolf. 2001. "Representative Bureaucracy and Harder Questions: A Response to Meier, Wrinkle, and Polinard." *Journal of Politics* 63:598–615.

Niskanen, William A. 1971. *Bureaucracy and Representative Government*. Chicago: Aldine.

———. 1975. "Bureaucrats and Politicians." *Journal of Law and Economics* 18:617–44.

———. 1991. "A Reflection on Bureaucracy and Representative Government." Pp. 13–31 in *The Budget-Maximizing Bureaucrat: Appraisals and Evidence*, edited by Andre Blais and Stephane Dion. Pittsburgh: University of Pittsburgh Press.

———. 1994. *Bureaucracy and Public Economics*. Brookfield, Vt.: Edward Algar Publishing.

Noll, Roger G. 1971. *Reforming Regulation*. Washington, D.C.: Brookings Institution.

Noll, Roger G., and Bruce Owen. 1983. *The Political Economy of Deregulation*. Washington, D.C.: American Enterprise Institute.

Peltzman, Sam. 1976. "Toward a More General Theory of Regulation." *Journal of Law and Economics* 19:211–40.

Perot, Ross. 1992. "An America That Reforms Its Politics." In *United We Stand: How We Can Take Back Our Country*. New York: Hyperion.

Perrow, Charles. 1986. *Complex Organizations: A Critical Essay*. New York: Random House.

Peters, B. Guy. 1984. *The Politics of Bureaucracy*. New York: Longman.

Pfiffner, James P. 1988. *The Strategic Presidency: Hitting the Ground Running*. Homewood, Ill.: The Dorsey Press.

Posner, Richard A. 1974. "Theories of Economic Regulation." *Bell Journal of Economics and Management Science* 5:337–52.

Potoski, Matthew. 2002. "Designing Bureaucratic Responsiveness: Administrative Procedures and Agency Choice in State Environmental Policy." *State Politics & Policy Quarterly*. 2:1–23.

Pratt, John W., and Richard J. Zeckhauser 1985. "Principals and Agents: An Overview." In *Principals and Agents: The Structure of Business*, edited by John W.

Pratt and Richard J. Zeckhauser. Cambridge, Mass.: Harvard Business School Press.

Pressman, Jeffrey L., and Aaron B. Wildavsky 1973. *Implementation.* Los Angeles: University of California Press.

Quirk, Paul J. 1981. *Industry Influence in Federal Regulatory Agencies.* Princeton: Princeton University Press.

Radner, Roy. 1985. "Repeated Principal-Agent Games with Discounting." *Econometrica* 53:1173–98.

Redford, Emmette S. 1969. *Democracy in the Administrative State.* New York: Oxford University Press.

Ringquist, Evan 1995a. "Political Control and Policy Impact in EPA's Office of Water Quality." *American Journal of Political Science* 39:336–63.

———. 1995b. "Environmental Protection Regulation." In *Regulation and Consumer Protection,* edited by Kenneth J. Meier and E. Thomas Garman. Houston: Dame Publications.

Ripley, Randall B., and Grace A. Franklin. 1986. *Policy Implementation and Bureaucracy.* Chicago: Dorsey Press.

Rogerson, William P. 1985. "The First-Order Approach to Principal-Agent Problems." *Econometrica* 53:1357–68.

Rossiter, Clinton. 1960. *The American Presidency.* New York: Harcourt, Brace, Jovanovich.

Rothman, Stanley, and S. Robert Lichter. 1983. "How Liberal are Bureaucrats?" *Regulation* 7:16–22.

Rourke, Francis. 1984. *Bureaucracy, Politics, and Public Policy.* 3d ed. Boston: Little, Brown.

Sabatier, Paul A., and Hank C. Jenkins-Smith. 1993. *Policy Change and Learning: An Advocacy Coalition Approach.* Boulder, Colo.: Westview.

Sabatier, Paul A., and Neil Pelkey. 1987. "Incorporating Multiple Actors and Guidance Instruments into Models of Regulatory Policy-making: An Advocacy Coalition Framework." *Administration and Society* 19:236–63.

Salisbury, Robert. 1969. "An Exchange Theory of Interest Groups." *Journal of Political Science* 13:1–32.

Sappington, Dave E. M. 1991. "Incentives in Principal-Agent Relationships." *Journal of Economic Perspectives.* 5:45–66.

Scher, Seymour. 1960. "Congressional Committee Members as Independent Agency Overseers: A Case Study." *American Political Science Review* 54:911–20.

Scholz, John T., and Feng Heng Wei. 1986. "Regulatory Enforcement in a Federalist System." *American Political Science Review* 80:1249–70.

Scholz, John T., Jim Twombly, and Barbara Headrick. 1991. "Street-level Political Controls Over Federal Bureaucracy." *American Political Science Review* 85:829–50.

Shapiro, Robert, and Harpreet Mahajan. 1986. "Gender Differences in Policy Preferences: A Summary of Trends from the 60s–80s." *Public Opinion Quarterly* 50:42–61.

Simon, Herbert 1946. "The Proverbs of Administration." *Public Administration Review* 6:53–67.

———. 1947. *Administrative Behavior*. New York: Free Press.

Sinclair-Desgagne, Bernard. 1994. "The First-Order Approach to Multi-Signal Principal-Agent Problems." *Econometrica* 62:459–65.

Singh, Nirvikar. 1985. "Monitoring Hierarchies: The Marginal Value of Information in a Principal-Agent Model." *Journal of Political Economy* 93:599–609.

Songer, Donald R., Jeffrey A. Segal, and Charles M. Cameron. 1994. "The Hierarchy of Justice: Testing a Principal-Agent Model of Supreme Court-Circuit Court Interactions." *American Journal of Political Science* 38:673–96.

SPSS. 1993. *SPSS Professional Statistics 6.1*. Chicago: Norusis/SPSS Inc.

Stehr, Steven D. 1997. "Top Bureaucrats and the Distribution of Influence in Reagan's Executive Branch." *Public Administration Review* 57:75–82.

Stevenson, William B. 1990. "Individual Discretion and Organizational Accountability: Evaluating the Performance of Public Bureaucrats." *Sociological Perspectives* 33:341–54.

Stewart, Joseph Jr., and Jane S. Cromartie. 1982. "Partisan Presidential Change and Regulatory Policy: The Case of the FTC and Deceptive Practices Cases." *Presidential Studies Quarterly* 12:586–73.

Stigler, George. 1970. "The Theory of Economic Regulation." *Bell Journal of Economics and Management Science* 2:3–21.

Stillman, Richard II. 1996. *The American Bureaucracy: The Core of Modern Government*. Chicago: Nelson-Hall Publishers.

Strauz, Roland. 1997. "Delegation of Monitoring in a Principal-Agent Relationship." *Review of Economic Studies* 64:337–57.

Stone, Alan. 1977. *Economic Regulation and the Public Interest: The Federal Trade Commission in Theory and Practice*. Ithaca, N.Y.: Cornell University Press.

Thomas, John Clayton. 1986. "The Personal Side of Street-Level Bureaucracy—Discrimination or Neutral Competence." *Urban Affairs Quarterly* 22:84–100.

Thompson, Frank, and Michael Scicchitano. 1987. "State Implementation and Federal Enforcement Priorities." *Administration and Society* 19:95–124.

Thompson, Victor A. 1975. *Without Sympathy or Enthusiasm: The Problem of Administrative Compassion*. Tuscaloosa, Ala.: University of Alabama Press.

Tomkin, Shelley Lynne. 1998. *Inside OMB: Politics and Process in the President's Budget Office*. Armonk, N.Y.: M. E. Sharpe.

Truman, David B. 1952. *The Governmental Process*. New York: Knopf.

Viscusi, W. Kip, and Richard J. Zeckhauser. 1979. "Optimal Standards with Incomplete Enforcement." *Public Policy* 27:437–56.

Volden, Craig. 2002. "A Formal Model of the Politics of Delegation in a Separation of Powers System." *American Journal of Political Science* 46:111–33.

Walker, Samuel. 1992. *The Police in America, an Introduction.* New York: McGraw-Hill.

Waterman, Richard W., 1989. *Presidential Influence and the Administrative State.* Knoxville: University of Tennessee Press.

———. 1999. "Bureaucratic Views of the President." Pp. 150–67 in *Presidential Policymaking: An End-of-Century Assessment,* edited by Steven A. Shull. Armonk, N.Y.: M. E. Sharpe.

Waterman, Richard W., and Jeff Gill. 2002. "Shirking Off Old Theories! A New Information Exchange Model of Principal-Agent Interaction." Paper presented at the Conference on State and Local Policy, Milwaukee.

Waterman, Richard W., Amelia Rouse, and Robert Wright. 1998. "The Venues of Influence: A New Theory of Political Control of the Bureaucracy." *Journal of Public Administration Research and Theory* 8:13–38.

Waterman, Richard W., and B. Dan Wood. 1992. "What Do We Do with Applied Research?" *PS: Political Science and Politics* (September): 559–64.

———. 1993. "Policy Monitoring and Policy Analysis" *Journal of Policy Analysis and Management* 12:685–99.

Waterman, Richard W., Robert L. Wright, and Gilbert St. Clair. 1999. *The Image-Is-Everything Presidency: Dilemmas in American Leadership.* Boulder, Colo.: Westview Press.

Weber, Max. 1946. *From Max Weber: Essays in Sociology.* Translated by H. H. Gerth and C. Wright Mills. New York: Oxford University Press.

Weingast, Barry, and Mark Moran. 1983. "Bureaucratic Discretion or Congressional Control: Regulatory Policy Making by the Federal Trade Commission." *Journal of Political Economy* 91:756–800.

West, William. 1983. "Institutionalizing Rationality in Regulatory Administration." *Public Administration Review* 43:326–34.

White, Leonard D. 1954. *The Jacksonians.* New York: Macmillan.

White, Theodore H. 1969. The Making of the President 1968: A Narrative History of American Politics in Action. New York: Atheneum Publishers.

Whitford, Andrew B. 2002. "Bureaucratic Discretion, Agency Structure, and Democratic Responsiveness: The Case of the United States Attorneys." *Journal of Public Administration Research and Theory* 12:3–27.

Wildavsky, Aaron. 1964. *The Politics of the Budgetary Process.* Boston: Little, Brown.

Will, George. 1993. "The Fatal Conceit." *Newsweek,* 8 March, 68.

Wilson, James Q. 1967. "The Bureaucratic Problem." *Public Interest* 6:3–9.

———. 1968. *Varieties of Police Behavior.* Cambridge, Mass.: Harvard University Press.

———. 1973. *Political Organizations.* New York: Basic Books.

———. 1975. "The Rise of the Bureaucratic State." *Public Interest* 41:77–103.

———. 1980. *The Politics of Regulation.* New York: Basic Books.

———. 1989. *Bureaucracy. What Government Agencies Do and Why They Do It.* New York: Basic Books.

Wilson, James Q., and John J. DiIulio. *American Government.* 7th ed. Boston: Houghton-Mifflin.

Wilson, Woodrow. 1987. "The Study of Administration." In *Classics of Public Administration,* edited by Jay M. Shafritz and Albert C. Hyde. Chicago: Dorsey Press.

Woll, Peter. 1963. *American Bureaucracy.* New York: Norton.

Wood, B. Dan. 1988. "Principals, Bureaucrats, and Responsiveness in Clean Air Enforcements." *American Political Science Review* 82:213–34.

———. 1990. "Does Politics Make a Difference at the EEOC?" *American Journal of Political Science* 34:503–30.

———. 1992. "Modeling Federal Implementation as a System: The Clean Air Case." *American Journal of Political Science* 36: 40–67.

Wood, B. Dan, and James E. Anderson. 1993. "The Politics of U.S. Antitrust Regulation." *American Journal of Political Science* 37:1–39.

Wood, B. Dan, and Richard Waterman. 1991. "The Dynamics of Political Control of the Bureaucracy." *American Political Science Review* 85:801–28.

———. 1993. "The Dynamics of Political-Bureaucratic Adaptation." *American Journal of Political Science* 37:497–528.

———. 1994. *Bureaucratic Dynamics. The Role of Bureaucracy in a Democracy.* Boulder, Colo.: Westview Press.

Worden, Robert E. 1984. "Patrol Officers Attitudes and the Distribution of Police Services: A Preliminary Study." Pp. 42–54 in *Understanding Police Agency Performance.* Washington, D.C.: U.S. Department of Justice, National Institute of Justice.

Yandle, Bruce. 1985. "FTC Activity and Presidential Effects." *Presidential Studies Quarterly* 15:128–35.

Yin, Robert K., and Douglas Yates. 1975. *Street-Level Governments Assessing Decentralization and Urban Services.* Lexington: Lexington Books.

INDEX